NEVER TRAVEL
in a Straight Line

Discovering Travel's True Purpose

Also, by Jim Menge:

Business Evangelism

NEVER TRAVEL
in a Straight Line

Discovering Travel's True Purpose

JIM MENGE

First Printing: 2023

ISBN 979-8-35093-309-3 paperback
ISBN: 979-8-35093-310-9 ebook

Ordering Information:
U.S. trade bookstores and wholesalers: Please email jim@jimmenge.com

Dedication

To the inner wanderer
who knows that the true journey lies not in the destination,
but in the path we take to get there.
and

Georgia Menge, mom
1926 - 2023

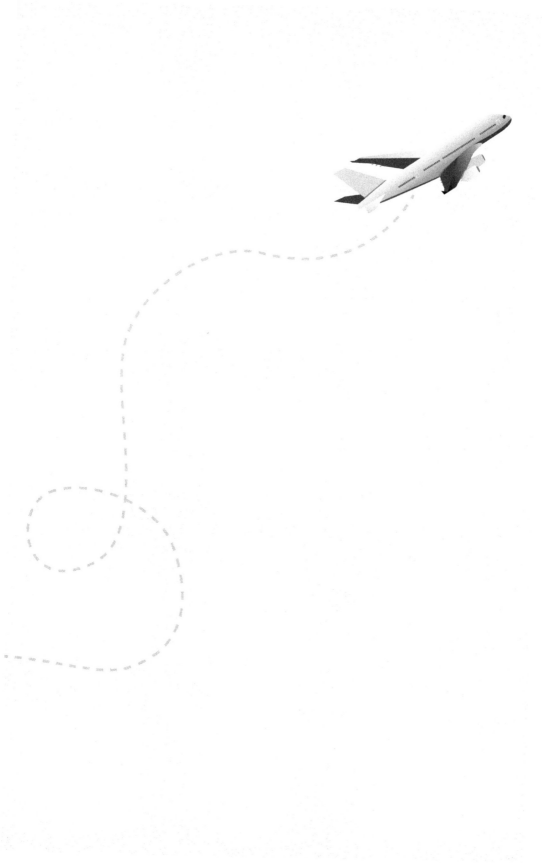

CONTENTS

ACKNOWLEDGMENTS

I want to thank those I've worked for and worked with. Many people fit this space, and each one matters.

Thank you to the people who have been part of this writing effort, beginning with Carole, who started me on the writing journey, encouraging me to compile the stacks of notes I was collecting.

Then, along the way came Zak, Chance, John, and Brad, who continued the journey with me. I am grateful for your insight, patience, and guidance. Each brought a unique perspective and contributed to my work.

Thank you to Caroline and Naghmeh for being honest and open and helping me navigate the Dark Nights. Caroline encouraged me to consider a different life narrative than the one I told myself. She said, "Turning the page of your journal is just surrendering to your thoughts." Naghmeh's counsel, "Jim, we're not solving for a sold-out audience of your fans." reminded me to stay humble, to be happy, and to not settle for good enough. I am a fan of them and waiting for their conference.

And finally, thank you to the people I've met on the road who are a part of this story.

FOREWORD

One of my earliest boarding passes is from a trip with my daughter to Paris. I remember sitting in the aisle seat, her by the window. I slept, she read. She was probably 13. A book, a Dr Pepper, some pretzels, a night light. That's all she needed. She brought a different book and shared a different perspective wherever we traveled.

She had traveled across the Atlantic several times and knew the routine. She'd been to London; we drove from Stockholm to Oslo and Madrid to Lisbon; we took the train from Paris to Zurich. We traveled across the U.S. many times.

I saw the world with new eyes through each of my two children. Travel took on a different perspective than when I traveled for business. I packed different clothes, traveled a different itinerary, ate different food, stayed at other hotels, and viewed each of my children as travel companions. I was happy to be with her on this trip.

I wrote a few thoughts, "When was the last time I did something for the first time?" It was a familiar quote, but one that I come back to repeatedly. My working title started as "Boarding Pass Epiphanies: Learnings of the Travelers' Life."

Epiphany is an elegant and tricky word at the same time. I wrote a chapter about epiphanies, and the rest of this book is what I collected over the years. This book is about learnings and moments of awareness while traveling, being conscious, and remaining active during travel. This book is about remembering.

A few years ago, at a conference, I spoke about what it is like to stand in line at the airport. The people we meet, a baby crying at 5 a.m., single travelers, couples, families, people in wheelchairs, people who are late and panicking, dogs, a cat, the lady with the pony, people happy or sad or nervous or anxious or numb. I talked about the security workers and who they must come across any day.

As I write this, and as is the case most years, travel over the winter holidays is messy. Planes are late; flights are canceled; snowstorms appear suddenly; crowds of infrequent travelers wander; computer systems fail; passengers bring more luggage than possible to put in the overhead bins, more bags than the luggage carousel can handle, lots of overcoats, wrap-around lines at Starbucks and Dunkin, out of BBQ at Austin airport, squatters at restaurants. It was almost heaven for me.

My phone buzzed with a message from an unknown caller. "Hi, Jim. U talked a few years ago about standing in line & how awesome the airport is. My hubby and I r spending two days at the airport, laughing our asses off because we never imagined we would be a part of it. T.Y."

As my daughter would say when something didn't go right, "Hey, Dad, c'est la vie."

Enjoy the journey.

PREFACE

Writing is tough.

Writing is challenging. For me, days and weeks would pass without writing a word. And sometimes, I would write for days, like traveling.

There are better writers. I write about them in this book. I appreciated the writing process. My writing did not seem perfect or finished. I didn't think of myself as someone who needed to drink to write or shut myself in a dark room like some I read about. I wrestled with the process, no doubt. I hope to give a different perspective on my profession and my passion.

Some travelers have been to more places, flown more miles, and board ahead of me. Tens of thousands of people sit on flights crisscrossing oceans and continents daily. Same plane, going to the same place. Even on a train crossing a country, a ship between ports, or a vehicle going to the same place. I'm happier to take the longer, slower, and windier road. I aim to show travelers they can have a richer experience by slowing down and paying attention.

There are motivators whose life work shows their audiences how having purpose leads to being different, achieving more, doing more, earning more, being more. That's OK, too. During my graduate studies, one of my favorite and go-to books is "A Swift Kick in the Pants." That was my motivation, something we all need from time to time. In this book, I aim for the reader to reach deeper and higher, to look around and inside themselves.

Travel writers have their way of connecting writing, travel, and purpose. While I attempt to be overt in my call to be aware and find meaning in travel, great travel writers and writers of travel create the dream and the drive. Mark Vanhoenacker, a British Airways Captain and author of Skyfaring and Imagine a City, is such a writer.

I write the way I speak as a storyteller. Punctuation notwithstanding, I hope that my writing style is easy to follow. Or as Sophie Grace Chappell writes in the Preface to her book, Epiphanies, An Ethics of Experience, *"I have had a wonderful three years–or ten–writing this book. I hope I am not the only one who enjoys it."*

And finally, there is the glue that brings it all together. This is Elizabeth Gilbert, specifically her audiobook, Big Magic: Creative Living Beyond Fear, and the related interview with Marie Forleo on YouTube. Seriously, just hearing Gilbert read her book is big magic.

"A creative life is an amplified life. It's a bigger life, a happier life, an expanded life, and a hell of a lot more interesting life. Living in this manner–continuously and stubbornly bringing for the jewels that are hidden within you–is a fine art, in and of itself."

–Elizabeth Gilbert, Big Magic

INTRODUCTION

Imperfection—welcome to the traveler's life.

Not written chronologically nor as a memoir, Never Travel in a Straight Line asks the traveler to bring their outward travel experience inward. Instead of blowing through a city, find something they can connect with, even for a day. Instead of a collection of Instagram photos, something imaginative. Instead of a soon-forgotten Facebook story, a story to tell long after the experience. Instead of a Tweet (or an X), a thunderbolt.

As a lifelong employee in the travel industry, I learned that travel happens in stages. These stages are:

- Dreaming: maybe a local drive or to a faraway destination. Or perhaps a cruise.

- Planning: considering the options, dates, and prices. According to Expedia, leisure travelers will visit thirty-four websites before they travel. That was a few years ago. I imagine it is more now.

- Reserving: committing.

- Waiting: the long period between Reserving and Traveling. Filling in the gaps, adding things to do or places to see, packing, and repacking.

- Traveling: the experience itself. Getting to the airport, train station, or cruise terminal. Moving. Being around other people. Delays.

Smells. Inconveniences. Feelings and emotions. Excitement. Taking pictures. Writing. Perhaps dreaming of the next trip.

- Returning: being something different from when you left. Remembering.

Purpose is an individual endeavor. I hope you, the reader, will indulge me in looking for your purpose on your next trip.

PART I:
WANDERING

I'M A TRAVELING MAN

I'm a Traveling Man.
I pack light, sit tight, and eat right.
I take the high road, side road, back road, and back alley.
I travel high, travel low, travel fast, travel slow.

I'm a traveling man with an end in mind... but not the end one would
easily find.
I make my own way, I make my own path, and at times, I fall ill to the
journey's wrath.
I'm a traveling man with a journey ahead, not seeking destinations waiting to
be tread.
To see, to share, to hear, to roll, to move is the key to feeding my soul.

I take the rough with the smooth when I'm roughing it,
or when the going gets rough, I get a little rough around the edges.
I'm a travel freak—an adventure geek who shares sneak peeks of
travel feats.
I'm a predestined, platinum-class mile seeker, preconditioned to pre-board.
I like a soft bed and a hard drink, but I settle for a soft drink and a hard bed.

I miss the red lights and catch the red eyes.
I'm packed up, picked up, action-packed, and been pickpocketed.
I've hit it off, hit the track, hit the bar, and hit the sack.
I take the long way home to make a short story long.

There are rules I follow when traveling abroad; I travel alone, unencumbered
and flawed.

I don't travel with bosses, colleagues, or friends; only those I know well and
can make quick amends.
I travel fast and with hardly a plan; I go with the flow and make up where
I can.
I change my mind, I change my speed, I change my way, I never concede.

I pack my things going out the door; a waste of time to pack before.
I've missed a flight, smelled a stench, slept in clothes on an airport bench.
I laugh and dance in the face of heat and rarely look back, never missing
a beat.
And once in a while, I score a treat and get to sit in an upgraded seat.

EPIPHANIES

"Something has to hurt to have an epiphany."

— Gwyneth Lloyd, Life Coach

I looked out the airplane window and saw a boy standing on his bicycle, leaning against the perimeter fence, watching our plane land.

Olympic Airways, Tel Aviv - Athens

If someone were going to have an epiphany, an excellent place to start would probably be the Holy Land—the genesis of Western faiths. It was here where I began this journey, and it was here where I went in search of an epiphany.

Not just any epiphany.

I traveled to Israel with my 16-year-old son, my sister and her family, and my Greek mother. After a lengthy period of relative peace in Israel, fighting between the inhabitants again broke out.

I had mixed feelings.

Would I return alive?

Would I lose my son?

Would there be another breakout of fighting?

Would I see the places where Abraham walked, where Jesus taught, and where Mohammed received his vision?

Could I see the Dome of the Rock and visit a mosque?

As a first-timer to the Holy Land, I did not visit lightly, not without some wonder, awe, or trepidation. At least not intentionally.

I expected the unexpected.

Was it unrealistic to expect the unexpected? The unexpected is, of course, just that—unexpected.

Arriving at different times and from different places, my family found each other in the somewhat chaotic customs entrance at one of the most locked-down airports in the world. We found ourselves halted by the ongoing and seemingly endless security, struck at the sight of 18-year-old guards with machine guns walking around as though it were natural to walk around anywhere with a machine gun and an endless barrage of questions. It all made for a safer experience.

Is there ever a good time to visit the Middle East? Conflicts among the earliest cultures have been going on since the first written word thousands of years earlier, as told by Susan Wise Bauer in her work, The History of the Ancient World: From the Earliest Accounts to the Fall of Rome.

We gathered our luggage. I gathered my thoughts.

The obvious was all around us. As a traveler relentlessly visiting uncommon places, I learned to stay aware of my surroundings. Most countries make traveling less problematic. Getting out of an international airport is a fairly straightforward experience:

Get off the plane. Wait.

Find the right line for Immigration. Wait.

Answer a question or two. Wait.

Find the luggage pickup. Wait.

Get your bags. Wait.

Walk through customs.

Walk out of the Arrivals doors.

Figure out the driver, taxi, train, bus, tour operator. Wait.

That's where the "normal" and "apparent" ends. Next, you're on your own. Pay attention.

We met our tour guide.

My sister, a travel agent, decided that we would hire a tour guide since there were seven of us. He called himself David. He had been through several wars and had two children. He knew as much about Americans and Palestinians as he did Israelis. He learned as much about Christianity and Islam as he did Judaism. It was his life and his job. It was also his passion.

We drove two hours from the Tel Aviv airport to Jerusalem. It looked like the drive between Las Cruces and Roswell in New Mexico. Desert. Hills. Something between hills and mountains. Desert fauna. Cacti. Shrubs. I imagined the stars shined bright at night with no lights around. Our guide dropped us off at our hotel.

That evening, we visited the old part of Jerusalem for dinner. We walked through narrow walkways. Stone buildings were everywhere with small doorways. We breathed dust.

I slipped into a different time, not like jet lag, but extra attentive. Travel does that. It makes us more aware and alert if we're fortunate; travel encourages us to let go of familiar things. Simple things like buying a cup of coffee and mentally converting money to see how much or how little something costs and seeing the differences in how people dress. I was hearing people speak unfamiliar languages. Hands were gesturing. More guards with machine guns. Each made me increasingly aware that I was not at home.

The next day, we visited Bethlehem, where Jesus was born. We touched the water where John the Baptist baptized Jesus. My mother bought several bottles of river (holy) water to bring home as a gift to the church and her priest. We walked outside the walls of Jerusalem, among the olive groves where David, the tour guide, suggested Jesus walked.

We drove by Jericho, where David told us of the wall that fell a couple of thousand years earlier, as though it had happened last year. We floated in the Dead Sea. We walked around the desert, maybe where Abraham built, and revisited the altars he left years before. We explored Masada, where the last of the Jewish holdouts stayed in 100 A.D. before being executed by the Romans.

We explored the streets of Jerusalem, where signs hung along the Twelve Stations of the Cross, the final path Jesus walked. We prayed at the Wailing Wall for peace and to be kept safe. We walked on the Temple Mount, built in place of Solomon's great temple.

David waited outside as we visited the Al-Aqsa Mosque. One of the Islamic holy sites, this is where Mohammed prayed, ascended to heaven, and spoke with God. While familiar with the faith, I was aware of the call to prayer made five times daily. We were told to wear decent clothing, including scarves for the women. We removed our shoes and walked behind those who were praying. I was in awe and inspired.

For a week, we lived and breathed the foundation of these faiths. I remember feeling in a daze. There was so much to experience from pieces of my upbringing, from friends I met over the years, and books I read.

As quickly as we arrived, it was time to leave. We drove the two hours back to the airport in Tel Aviv.

David and I discussed tourism since I worked in the travel industry. I asked how he felt about tourists and their expectations, good or bad. He responded that there were more expectations than he could name. "Many came as their lifelong dream. Some found a new life. Some learned. Some changed. Some left feeling cheated."

He said, "What people expected the most but couldn't put into words was that finding an epiphany eluded them."

An epiphany? An awakening? A miracle? A revelation? An "AHA" moment?

His response awakened something in me.

Did I have an epiphany?

Did I miss it?

Quickly, I considered what I saw, where I went, and what I heard while visiting the holy places. I felt my education and upbringing. I reflected on my need for meaning.

Was I being aware?

Was I conscious?

Epiphanies may happen in the subconscious, as in a dream.

I was in Israel. I traveled. I took planes, buses, trains, boats, ferries, and cars. I walked. I fell. I got back up. I got stuck. I got back on. I got lost. I found my way. I was sad. I was happy.

A reviewer of The Innocents Abroad by Mark Twain wrote, *"Mark Twain, cynical about so much else, has a particular reverence in the Holy Land for 'sitting where a god has stood.' What flabbergasted him was that his traveling companions would be in such a sanctified environment and winter what they saw according to other writers or their denominational background instead of their own experience with the holy."*

As we arrived back at the airport, I realized my journey had begun long before I realized it, and this was a stop along the way.

I had an epiphany.

TAKE AWAY: A breakthrough is when we move through some blockage or something holding us back. There is a point of inflection and movement. Breakthroughs happen personally and professionally. Personal breakthroughs involve relationships, where to live, and what to do.

Professional breakthroughs include determining which work matters, solutions to stalled projects, and innovation awakenings.

BOARDING PASSES

American Airlines, Dallas–Paris

Can travel be something where we can experience the unexpected?

100%.

No doubt.

Absolutely.

And you don't even have to try.

Get on a train, a plane, or a ship, and sit back. The unexpected unfolds and happens. All by itself. The unexpected is exhilarating and transformative but is also exhausting and irritating. But that's not the point.

And yet, that is precisely the point.

It's the irritant that makes the pearl. It's the irritant that causes the memory. And it's the irritant that makes the story. One of the more famous contemporary quotes of the travel story is from an interview with famed travel writer Paul Theroux, who said, *"Travel is glamorous only in retrospect."* Pain is undoubtedly one aspect of the traveler's memory. We've been there, and we each have stories of trips that went from bad to worse, many times starting before we left our house!

As part of my work at a leading travel company, I interviewed a hundred of the top U.S. travel consultants. Ranked annually in magazines, including Conde Nast Traveler, National Geographic Traveler, and Travel & Leisure, these travel consultants knew their destinations better than any. They created memorable encounters for even the most ardent traveler.

My goal was to understand why they are the best, the most knowledgeable, and how they achieved the near impossible for their clientele. They explained their airline and hotel knowledge, destination experience, partnership networks, and relationships. They spoke about their love of traveling, spending time with whatever their specialty is, and spending as much time as it took to be the best. They knew the chef at the leading hotel and which restaurants would be suitable for their clients. At a hotel site inspection, they imagined which room would be perfect for a specific client on a special occasion, such as an anniversary or birthday.

I asked about their clients in greater detail. Indeed, there were aspects of insurmountable travel requirements. These travel consultants rose to the task and performed feats that rose above the Internet. They told me about one, two, or three clients seeking something more. Money was no object.

What mattered was the experience. Pain or not. The extent that some travelers would go through to have a "trip of a lifetime" once, then twice, then again piqued my interest. The ongoing drive consumed these travelers.

It is a bit of an oxymoron to have more than one "trip of a lifetime." I get it. But how do we get more out of travel than simply a trip or even a "trip of a lifetime?"

I've been fortunate to have had a few trips of a lifetime. William Shatner blasted into the atmosphere aboard an Amazon rocket, the trip of a lifetime for sure, and his response was, *"I want to do it again."*

I work in an industry and have jobs leading and managing the creation of traveler experiences. They are different for everyone. From the cadence of business travel to the never-traveled people to the "trip of a lifetime" people—those who cannot afford a trip but travel to the people with endless cash. Money does not denote happiness or unhappiness with travel. I know. I've met them both.

Travel could be existential, leaving friends and families behind, as my mother did without returning to her country for 30 years, or, as my grandmother did, never to return to her homeland. Travel can be about starting new lives and about returning. I wrote about why we travel in an article, "The Traveler Hierarchy, a sort of Maslow's Hierarchy of Needs." My version was for travelers.

Travel comes in all shapes and sizes: business travel, event travel, leisure travel, family travel, and multi-generational travel. Those excited and those afraid. Those happy and those sad. Each has their own experience. Some share their experience with others, like it or not.

Let's go back to the question at the beginning of this chapter, "Is travel something we can experience the unexpected?" Is travel something we can do that creates stories and memories to make us better, to make the world better? Can we hit the brakes on where we're heading to find the path that awakens and enlivens us?

I believe so.

Is it guaranteed?

No, but we can come close.

The boy, Santiago, in The Alchemist, had several epiphanies. Toward the end of the book, after years of searching for his treasure, he is exhausted and ready to quit. Then, with a stroke of insight, he dug all night where he believed he would find the treasure.

But then, attackers showed up, forcing him to dig more, dig harder, and dig faster.

"They made the boy continue digging, but he found nothing. As the sun rose, the men began to beat the boy. He was bruised and bleeding, his clothing torn to shreds, and he felt that death was near." After they left, *"The boy stood up shakily and looked once more at the Pyramids. They seemed to laugh at him, and he laughed back, his heart bursting with joy. Because now he knew where his treasure was."*

The boy traveled for years and thousands of miles to have the epiphany leading him to his treasure. What happened?

Elise Ballard is the author and curator of Epiphany: True Stories of Sudden Insight to Inspire, Encourage and Transform. She expands on the definition of epiphany: "*A moment of great or sudden revelation that usually changes your life in some way.*"

Jerry McGuire had an epiphany. Tired and disillusioned with his work, he wrote a 35-page mission statement. (Talk with me if you ever need a 35-page mission statement. I can help get it down to one page).

Then, after presenting his mission statement, his boss fired him. Classic.

Elise Ballard interviewed 58 well-known people who had epiphanies. She writes about each of their transformational moments. As Ballard discusses in her TEDx talk, an epiphany is an "Aha moment." It may hit you on the spot or days, weeks, or months later. It is a defining moment.

I've had lots of epiphanies while traveling. Some of the best ones. Some are exhausting. Others are simple, like a 5 a.m. flight while the 20-something lady beside me vomited. She was pregnant, scared, tired, and going to visit her military husband. She just needed someone to tell her it would be "OK." I finally understood compassion.

An eight-year-old boy just wanted to sit by the window where I sat. I saw my eagerness in him. I asked a lost, elderly woman in Atlanta to "hold" a table for a colleague and me while we grabbed dinner for the three of us. I would want the same for my mother, son, or daughter. I understood seeing something again for the first time.

Epiphanies help us see what we're missing.

There are few times when I travel that as the plane lands, the train pulls into a station, or the ship pulls into a port when I am not awestruck.

I travel to make epiphanies.

I experience epiphanies.

I live epiphanies.

I write about epiphanies.

I talk about epiphanies.

Travel can create epiphanies.

And, as Elise Ballard writes, *"The epiphany finds you when you're ready."*

TAKE AWAY: The more we feed into memories and activities that move us toward a goal, the more excellent the opportunity will be to find the unexpected. In my innovation management work, we learn to unpack the assumptions to set the innovation free. Work and our personal lives can be challenging at times. It is through these times that we know what our abilities, tendencies, likes and dislikes, strengths and weaknesses are all about.

MAPS & PLACES

American Airlines, Chicago–Shanghai

"A map is the greatest of all epic poems. Its lines and colors show the realization of great dreams."

– Gilbert Grosvenor

I'm a map guy.

We could drive around the block, and I'll have the GPS and my iPhone navigation running.

I look for maps wherever I go.

I study the streets, look for other routes, and see if roads have recently changed. I look for the unique and unusual, generally travel or historically related. Driving cross country, I look for airports. Old airports. Old train stations. Anything that screams, "Progress happened here."

Maps show history. They show progress (or regress). They show rivers, mountains, shorelines, railroad lines, airports, cities, lakes, and deserts. As a private pilot, I learned to read aviation maps that showed the landscape and where I could and couldn't fly.

As a kid, I collected airline maps to see all the places the airlines flew. I learned about country and city names. Some maps were in other languages, so I had to refer to the World Book Encyclopedia (a word we don't hear enough of these days) in the Dark Ages before the Internet. My father had maps of places he'd visited and Navy books with other maps.

AAA gave out a Triptik, a plastic spiral-bound booklet with all the roadside motels and dinosaur parks to visit on your family drive. That's how my father drove six of us from Miami to New York for a two-week vacation. He smoked. We gagged. "Are we there yet?" Yes, there was a communal pee bottle. With four boys, it just happened. I followed the map.

Some airlines have moving maps to show where you are.

As we left Chicago for Shanghai, the plane on the moving map headed north. I was on this flight because my visa to visit China was in a different passport (with me), but not the passport I was traveling on. A disagreement with the ticket counter agent about the validity of my visa (yes, it was still valid, but arguing with the ticket counter agent was not the solution) rendered me missing my flight (which would have happened since the United Airlines Visa-Checking person did not start work until 8 a.m.), so I wound up flying via Chicago.

There was a slight turn here and there, but overall, we just traveled up (north). A few hours later, I could see that we were heading for the North Pole. As we got closer, the plane on the map stopped moving, and the map started turning. A few hours later, the plane on the map was pointing left and then down (south). We headed toward Siberia, missed Mongolia, and turned toward Shanghai.

I loved seeing it on a map.

Flying across the Atlantic, I look to see how close to Iceland and Greenland we will fly. On flights from London to Los Angeles, we fly over Iceland and Greenland. The icebergs and ice floes look so large and seem close enough that I felt I could touch them. When traveling across the ocean, I get a seat on the north side of the trip since it is more scenic.

Another perspective was taking the Queen Mary 2 from New York to London across the Atlantic Ocean. The captain gave us a daily update on how deep the water was, the deepest point, as we passed near the Titanic and officially passed from North America to the European continent. I stared at the map in my cabin for eight days.

After walking across Spain, we flew south from Madrid to Miami. I noticed the brown Sahara Desert over the northern half of Africa. Straight west was the green rainforest of the Amazon and Central America.

From London to Nairobi, our plane flew south over Europe, the Mediterranean, the Sahara Desert, and the jungles of East Africa. The Earth was taking care of itself.

When traveling to Japan, co-workers in the U.S. who were less enthusiastic about traveling long distances asked if I would "stop by" to visit their customers in Hong Kong. I replied, "Yes, as long as you visit my customers in Los Angeles when you are next in New York." It was roughly the same distance. They didn't get the joke.

I find map stores wherever I travel and when I am not in a bookstore. I frequent map stores in Southern California, San Francisco, Miami, New York, London, antique stores, or wherever I can find old maps. Who knew that, in 1900, less than 500 people lived in Fort Dallas—an orange grove renamed to Miami several years later? Stanfords and Daunt Books in London are my favorites. They are a pilgrimage unto themselves.

And the older the map, the better. I have old maps and atlases from the 1800s showing Hindustan instead of India and Pakistan, and Russia owning Alaska. Britain colonized British Honduras, British East Africa, British Somaliland, and British West Indies because Eddie Izzard says, *"The British showed up with a flag."*

And what of Spain-controlled Sahara, which seemed to be half of northwest Africa before the United Nations renamed it Western Sahara in 1975? There's supposed to be a freight train that rolls through there; that sounds like an adventure.

At one time, Bolivia touched the Pacific Ocean, and Colombia stretched into Panama before the canal. Places existed, like Ceylon and the Sandwich Islands.

Tanganyika is Tanzania. The airport code, PEK for Peking, is now Beijing. Canton, CAN, is Guangzhou. Ceylon is Sri Lanka. Siam is Thailand. In 2022, Turkey became Türkiye.

Maps give a perspective of size and time. The world is getting smaller, but it is still enormous. The world is changing, but the people are still the people. The places are still magical.

I'm a map guy. The older, the better.

Not me. The maps.

P.S. Gilbert Grosvenor, the guy I quoted at the beginning of this piece, was the first editor of National Geographic Magazine. He became the president of the National Geographic Society in 1920.

TAKE AWAY: Maps are visual. This could look like writing out the pros and cons of a problem. Professionally, it isn't until I present a visual chart to my clients showing the path from the current state to the final solution that they gain understanding and confidence in the delivery. Maps give perspective.

PLACES

American Airlines, Quito-Miami

When people learn I've traveled to over 100 countries, they ask me which is my favorite. My response has something to do with saying that each place is special or unique and affected me differently or "the next place."

Many times, as I revisited a place, it affected me differently. The same is true when traveling with others or for different purposes. Many factors go into a favorite place.

I love South and Central America. Many large cities there, like São Paulo, Buenos Aires, Lima, Quito, Bogota, and Panama City, still feel like they would have in the 1950s and 1960s. Majestic churches, immense government buildings and schools, plazas in the town squares, and wide streets paint a much slower pace for those with an all-too-rapidly changing lifestyle. Visiting each city forces a sense of a slower pace.

Like Miami, a Spanish city with painstaking detail around architecture, street names, ornate woodwork, stucco, and color, I felt at home in most South American cities I visited. As I walked the streets of these cities, I imagined the glamour from when the buildings were being built, including the Pan Americano Hotel in Buenos Aires.

London is cool. Huge. Super huge. While London is one of the most advanced cities in the world, many buildings are still hundreds of years old. The contrast between old and new is real. Not only the architecture, but much of the world also views London as a part of their heritage, making travel to London almost a pilgrimage. On a recent trip, a colleague and I traveled about London via the waterways as they would have done one or two hundred years ago. After many trips to London, seeing the city from the water was almost an epiphany of its own.

The same applies to Amsterdam, Brussels, Paris, Madrid, Lisbon, and Rome. The architecture, languages and dialects, customs, and beliefs rippled from these cities to countries worldwide. This ripple continues because of extraordinary travel abilities, language learning, and global economics. To see a people's culture in real-time and to have visited the place of lineage from just a few hundred years previous makes the world seem smaller.

The people—their passion, hard work, play, and hearing them laugh- are all part of a place. With most people, what matters most is their happiness and their story. Listening to someone's story is like a breath that turns the world. The effort many spent to get where they are, along with the stories of their parents, grandparents, and great-grandparents, continue to build pathways of progress. Their stories are compelling. Their stories speak of places.

The same applies to those traveling and moving within a country or region. In the U.S., people are moving from New York and New Jersey to Florida and Arizona, from London to Cyprus, and from Amsterdam to Malaga, where it is warmer. Multi-generational families live and travel together. A place is always rooted in its people. New Orleans is one of the best examples of an area forming and maintaining a mixed culture over hundreds of years, mainly from Africa, France, and Spain. As people move, the world evolves.

I listen to older adults and their stories. I study the deep lines on their faces, reminders for me of my parent's friends who visited from the old country.

In Quito, Ecuador, I walked into the Iglesia de la Compañía with a customer I had met a month earlier at a sales conference. When I arrived in Quito, my client took me from place to place. In South America, like other parts of the business world, relationships are essential and often outlast whatever business partnership brought them together.

My client, a successful Spanish business owner, was impressive and respected in the workplace. Often, business transactions occur outside of the office. In Japan, they transact many business deals at night in restaurants or bars. In Belgium, we discussed work and non-work topics during the day and at dinner. In Canada, what happened at the hockey game mattered as much, if not more, than what they said at the office. And, in Paris, dinner was pivotal.

Status still matters in many places, although it may be obscure. In Japan, how you hand someone a business card, where people sit around a table, and how you eat sushi still matters. South Americans have specific finesse in business dealings, like keeping the process in sequence. The size of one's office, the respect shown during discussions, the restaurants where one ate, the car - each was intentional. And since I was not from South America and did not speak Spanish well, nor Japanese or Portuguese, people were always helpful—especially when I attempted to speak their language.

In Ecuador, I visited La Mitad del Mundo ("The Middle of the World"), marking the Equator with a long yellow line. I straddled the line, traveling 1,000 miles (1,670 kilometers) per hour, the Earth's rotational speed. I grew up thinking that wherever the Equator was, it was hot, but since Quito was 9,000 feet (2,850 meters) high, the temperature was cool. That day, it was nearly freezing. Later, I would visit the Equator in Kenya and Indonesia.

The Equator reminded me of other unique places. Visiting Machu Picchu, we flew to Cuzco, Peru. The plane landed through the clouds at 11,000 feet (3,400 meters). This should have indicated insufficient oxygen because of the altitude. We made it to our chalet, where the proprietors encouraged us to rest and acclimate.

I lay in bed, watching my lungs move, except no air was going in or out. It reminded me of the flight attendant explaining that the airbag, when you place it over your nose and mouth in an emergency, will not inflate. I studied this craziness like I was having an out-of-body experience. The chalet owners came by and dropped off cocoa leaves for us to chew, which calmed our nerves. Who knew?

Back in Lima, the capital of Peru, I felt suffocated in the catacombs under the Basilica and Convent of San Francisco of Lima. Seventy thousand people are buried there, their bones lined up in patterns of varying types. The catacombs were otherworldly and became more known for their history and maze of passageways.

The guide let us explore on our own. Possibly, some of those people, from the bones, got lost. Then, I imagined I must have run out of oxygen in a previous life, and my anxiety got worse. The guide had me lie down. When I turned my head and saw the bones beside me, my fear sped into overdrive. It's not a place to get lost or locked up for the night.

My son and I took the train to Lhasa a few years later. Getting to Tibet by train is part of the process. Traveling as high as 16,000 feet (5,000 meters), they supplement the train cars with oxygen. I thought I was having a religious experience, but it was another lack of oxygen episode.

While working in Santiago, Chile, I stayed the weekend. After several suggestions, I visited the driest place on Earth and one of the most magical places I've seen, the Atacama Desert. Traveling with a colleague, we stayed at a rustic inn next to the church. In the morning, my head throbbed; I thought it was from being so dry there. I realized there was a parade, and my room shared a wall with the church, from which someone was beating a drum.

I walked outside to see what was happening. The parade leader lassoed and made me a part of a parade. I just wanted my headache to end. Since I did not understand Spanish, I went along with the program and was pulled into the courtyard, still just wearing my socks. Years later, I learned that the parade is part of a week-long Fiesta de San Pedro y San Pablo festival. I met some great people and began to practice being more discrete.

Over the past several years, the travel industry has created initiatives to better care for the places and people where tourists and travelers visit. These places and people are necessary for travelers to broaden their global awareness, increase their learning and tolerance, and support the local economies.

I left Quito the next day—a cold equator, a hot place, and warm people.

TAKE AWAY: We can use places to break the status quo. Even within our workplace, we can create new ways of broadening our perspective. As an executive, I enjoyed visiting staff members in their cubicles to discuss project issues and solutions. It was different than meeting in a conference room or office. I wanted to show each person value and visit them in "their" place with their pictures and uniqueness.

NOISE

American Airlines, New York - Dallas

Noise is just a part of travel. And noise, like a place, is unique.

Noise is different in different parts of the world. Horn sounds are different. Siren sounds are different. Telephone ring sounds are different. Accents are different. Animal noises are pronounced differently.

Some places are noisier than others.

New York City, Manhattan, is a noisy place. With three million people in a twenty-square-mile area daily, there is going to be noise: taxis, people, horns, sirens, cars moving, trucks backing-up noise, signal light sounds for the seeing impaired, ATMs, more trucks, dumpsters, garbage trucks, people talking, people yelling, people yelling at me, and cell phones ringing before they could vibrate.

And all before breakfast.

I was visiting New York for work. Sloshing through the snow, I took refuge at the Frontier Coffee Shop at E39th and 3rd. I sat across from an older couple and ordered a cup of coffee. The server brought it in a ceramic mug - the white ceramic mug typical at diners—the white ceramic cup that is permanently brown inside after years of use. Perfect.

And then, in slow motion, the old guy stirs his coffee with his metal spoon, and the clinking sound begins.

Clink

Clink

Clink

For a minute and a half, he was in a daze.

And when he's finished, his wife starts.

Clink

Clink

Clink

She, too, was paying attention to something else.

By now, I found that listening to the noise was melodic, even amusing. I found myself in a trance. The noise was everywhere: in the restaurant, on the streets, and certainly in my head.

I've read about people who can pick out individual sounds among the noise - the sound of a cricket chirping two blocks away. I saw that in a movie once. The sound of a coin (another relic of the past) hitting the ground, a cane tapping on the sidewalk, or people talking.

The subway has its unique noise. No one really can understand the announcements. As the metal train rail slides along the overhead electric line, the trains make metal wheel sounds on metal rails. Doors open and close. People swear as the subway train pulls away from the station, leaving them behind.

In the taxi, a commercial is playing on the T.V. asking if I want to buy tickets to a Broadway show. Or the news is on. Or, in the Uber, the driver wants to talk. Or play loud music. Or, hopefully, Howard Stern, the king of all media.

I go to my meeting. Some guy has his phone keyboard on click mode, so we can hear him typing during my presentation. We hear the noise outside, which is more like a background effect. We're saturated and unmindful at the same time.

It reminded me of working in the telecommunications field in the Air Force. The phone lines were so quiet that someone invented "white noise" so the listener wouldn't think the other person had hung up on them.

That evening at the airport, as I waited for my plane home, the flights were all delayed several hours because of the snowy weather. Christmas music was playing over the speaker. People complained that it was too loud.

I walked to the end of the concourse, where my flight was supposed to depart, and found hundreds of people waiting. I put my roll-aboard on the ground and sat on it, leaning against the wall. It was going to be a long evening.

The announcements came and went. Gates changed. The music was tiring. People were exhausted. Some were talking, sharing their 'disaster' stories of what the delays would cause. Others continued complaining—some loudly.

Like the guy listening to a cricket in the city, you could hear a single cell phone ringing. It got louder and louder. People started looking for where the sound was coming from. They were talking less and less. Then another cell phone rang. Then another.

Sitting across from me was an aged lady who had just received her first cell phone. Sitting in her chair in the middle of hundreds of people, she tried one ringtone after another. And since she was hard of hearing, she turned the volume to its loudest setting. The Verizon tone, the Microsoft tone, the Nokia tone, the old-fashioned ringtone—one by one—nice and loud.

I sat watching, listening, and smiling.

With each ringtone tryout, a different set of people grabbed their cell phones since they had set their ringer to whatever ringtone the lady was trying.

Over and over.

Melodic, the noise was priceless.

TAKE AWAY: Noise and sounds shift awareness. Consider when a cell phone makes an unexpected noise during a conversation and meeting. Or when a usually silent person speaks up. Noises want to be heard, like the bear in the woods.

BAGGAGE-ACTUALLY
AND METAPHORICALLY

Alaska Airlines, Fairbanks - Barrow
Alaska Airlines, Juneau - Anchorage

> *"All of us, when we travel, look at the places we go, the things
> we see, through different eyes. And how we see them is
> shaped by our previous lives, the books we've read, the films
> we've seen, the baggage we carry."*

Excerpt From: Anthony Bourdain. World Travel.

Me: A.A.: LAX DFW MEX LA: MEX SCL IPC (stop) LA: IPC SCL QF: SCL
SYD 3K: SYD OOL (stop) 3K: OOL SYD MH: SYD KUL (stop) CX: KUL
HKG (stop) CX: HKG AKL AA: AKL LAX

My Luggage: LAX MEX SCL IPC PPT (stop) IPC SCL LAX (stop)

I rarely checked luggage under the plane for most of my traveling life. First, as
an airline employee, I was never 100% certain that I would board any specific
flight. Then, as a paying passenger, all kinds of other scenarios happened.
Flight cancellations were common. Traveling outside of the country posed
other problems. The weight of the bags became a factor, so I carried a small
foldable cloth bag inside my suitcase to put things in when overweight.

A plane I traveled on from Colombia to the U.S. carried extra cargo, so the
airline reduced the number of passengers to meet the aircraft's weight requirements. Sometimes, headwinds require reducing plane weight because the

plane must carry extra fuel. A few times, gate agents asked me to deplane with my luggage to put me on a more direct flight, and because I did not check my bags, I could jump into the last seat of another flight at the last minute.

And then, one day, I tired of being a business traveler getting to the airport earlier so I could spend a couple of hours in the airline lounge eating lousy food, pissed off at parents on their phone whose honor roll kids were running around like animals, shoving through crowds waiting to board so I could find space for my luggage overhead, and then sit there watching people trying to push their oversized luggage in the overhead over my head.

On a flight from Beijing to Chicago, I got to my seat only to find crew luggage in the overhead compartments for three rows! I asked the flight attendant if the crew member could move their luggage. A minute later, a pilot showed up, letting me know it was his luggage. He asked, "If there would be a problem." I could have argued and possibly been removed from the aircraft, so it wasn't worth it. A new generation of crew and passengers was making travel less fun.

I started checking my bag. And I learned a few things about luggage and baggage.

Baggage Adds Levels of Complexity - Actually and Metaphorically

Here's what I've learned in millions of miles of flying over thousands of flights about the baggage we carry:

Some people have more baggage than others do. You can see it in their face.

Some people don't have any baggage. They are light.

Some people carry more baggage than they need or than they can manage. They are definitely stressed.

Some people inherit their baggage. Old and tired.

Some people have the entire collection, while others have a mishmash of baggage. Disjointed.

Some people wrap their baggage in plastic wraps or covers, like baggage inside of baggage. Not even lovely baggage. You can see through whatever is trying to cover what is inside.

Some people have ratty baggage. Maybe it's all they know.

I've seen heavy baggage, although you can't tell with the newfangled metal bags nowadays. What we know about baggage nowadays and in the past has changed.

Some people have expensive baggage. They are proud of it. They spent a lot of money on it. They defend it. They tell you what their expensive baggage means to them. They put plastic over it.

Some people pay to take extra baggage. A lot extra.

Unfortunately, some people's baggage gets lost or stolen and broken into. I feel bad for them, standing in long lines, lost, wondering what to do (that happened to me when I started writing this chapter).

Indeed, some baggage is for long hauling.

Some baggage recurs, carried over and over. You see it wherever you go.

Some people have substantial baggage. Nothing will break it. Indestructible. Made to withstand anyone else's baggage or from getting tossed around.

Some people have the same baggage. Nowadays, most people have the same baggage. I see it on Social Media.

In the old days, they had trunks. Or nothing.

Your Baggage Tells a Story - Actually and Metaphorically.

Paul Theroux dedicates a chapter, "The Things They Carried," in his book, The Tao of Travel, to what people carry as baggage. He retells his meeting with a Buddhist Monk whose entire baggage was a square cloth fashioned into a bag. I read his books to find out what Theroux carries on his months of travels to look inconspicuous. On his trip from Cairo to Cape Town, in his book, Dark

Star Safari, he writes about buying local second-hand clothes so he doesn't stand out as a tourist. There was hardly any baggage involved.

After the airline job, I learned to pack only what I needed. That is what I carried aboard with me.

My motto was, "If you can't carry it, you can't bring it." This became a speed exercise—not dealing with the ticket counter before my flight nor waiting for luggage upon arrival. On arrival, this could be thirty to forty-five minutes. Carrying my luggage aboard was faster since most of my travel was a day or two. Get to the airport, go through security, stow my bag, get off, get a cab or car, and go.

Ryan Bingham (George Clooney) sums up checked baggage to a colleague in the movie Up in the Air. *"Know how much time you lose by checking in? Thirty-five minutes a flight. I travel 270 days a year. That's 157 hours. That makes seven days. Are you willing to throw away an entire week on that?"*

Baggage is the Opposite of Speed - Actually and Metaphorically.

Some trips are multiple-segment and multi-hemispheric. Sometimes, a carry-on bag won't do it.

I had the following two-week itinerary on this trip, including new places, new routes, and lower prices. All in June. Not a straight line:

Portion 1: Los Angeles, California - Dallas-Fort Worth, Texas - Mexico City, Mexico (American Airlines)- Santiago, Chile - Easter Island, Chile (LAN). My son met me, and we spent a few days on Easter Island. Great place. Middle of nowhere. Go, just because it is remote.

Portion 2: Easter Island, Chile - Santiago, Chile - Auckland, New Zealand - Sydney, NSW Australia - Gold Coast, Queensland, Australia. I had business meetings. This "don't travel in a straight line" makes all the difference.

Portion 3: Gold Coast, Queensland, Australia - Sydney, NSW Australia - Kuala Lumpur, Malaysia for client meetings.

Portion 4: Kuala Lumpur, Malaysia - Hong Kong for company meetings.

Portion 5: Hong Kong - Auckland, New Zealand - Santiago, Chile - Los Angeles, California, for my return home.

Here's the deal. This could have cost over $8,000 in economy class, but my son figured out how to buy it all on LAN Airlines (based in Chile, in South America) for about the same price and fly in business class. Flying the straight-line route would cost two or three times—and boring.

In June, north of the Equator is hot. Kuala Lumpur, Malaysia, and Hong Kong are north of the Equator. And humid. Especially Kuala Lumpur. Outside is an instant body drench from the airport terminal to the car.

In June, south of the Equator is cold, needing more than a short-sleeved cotton shirt. Chile, New Zealand, and Australia would probably be chilly—not freezing, but for a week-long trip, cold enough to pack some long-sleeved shirts.

I needed extra clothes for both climates. My travels prevented hotel laundry since I arrived late and left early within a day or two. By traveling via Chile, I got a fantastic rate, flew in business class, and added Easter Island, also in business class, for $200 extra.

Sometimes, Baggage is Inevitable - Actually and Metaphorically.

I was strategic since I had a diverse itinerary ahead of me. I packed half of my clothing in a carry-on and the other half to be checked. Half of my cold weather clothes were in each. Half of my warm weather clothes were in each. Half of my underclothes are in each. Half of my socks are in each, all black. One pair of shoes is in each. Extra liquids went into the checked bag.

Own Your Baggage. Don't Let Your Baggage Own You - Actually and Metaphorically.

The bag I checked underneath to Easter Island went to Tahiti (Portion 1), which, unfortunately, was not on my itinerary. When we cleared customs and got to the luggage belt, the thrice-weekly Boeing 787 departed with my carry-on bag. I felt good about what I carried onboard, so I filled out and signed the triplicate lost baggage form. The airline representative assured me my baggage would be on my return flight from Tahiti the next day.

Except it wasn't. My bag stayed in Tahiti.

Sometimes, What You're Told About Your Baggage Isn't What It Is - Actually or Metaphorically.

I returned to the airport with lost baggage forms in hand the next day. The baggage representative was friendly, although unable to help. They had just confirmed that my bag was still in Tahiti. The best solution was that they could send it to me on my journey. This seemed worse since I did not understand how six airlines would keep track of my baggage around the Pacific Rim.

Your Baggage is Your Problem, Not Someone Else's Problem - Actually and Metaphorically.

I almost always see someone or a family repacking their bags at check-in. It's expensive when baggage is overweight, so they open it up, sort through things, and put the items in another bag. Or they wear it.

In Santiago, I resolved the airline would hold my bag in Santiago and return it to me in Los Angeles on my return ten days later. I boarded my connection to Auckland and on to Sydney.

Halfway over the Pacific, a passenger died. The plane turned around to return to Santiago. When we arrived, we were told to join the next flight in about 24 hours.

In a Diversion, Less Baggage is Better - Actually and Metaphorically.

Waiting 24 hours would not work for me, so I cashed in my ticket for a nonstop flight to Sydney on another airline, leaving in six hours. I reserved a hotel room, took a shower and a nap, returned to the airport, customs, and immigration, and ran to the gate. Had I had checked baggage, this scenario would not have been possible.

Baggage Can Slow Down Opportunities - Actually and Metaphorically.

Other than my baggage dealings, my trip went well. Meetings in Australia, Malaysia, and Hong Kong were significant. However, as frequent travelers know, schedules change. My return flight from Hong Kong to Auckland ran late, causing me to miss my flight from Auckland to Santiago. I could wait, but the thrice-weekly flight from Auckland to Santiago would only be there for a few more days. I love New Zealand, but I have a desk job I needed to get back to. I had made it through my trip with half my belongings by now. I bought the things I needed and managed with what I had.

Sometimes, We Learn Too Late That We Carry Too Much Baggage - Actually and Metaphorically.

When I arrived in Auckland, the airline moved me to a nonstop flight back to Los Angeles, and I skipped the South American route. To be sure, Santiago is a world-favorite city for me. The airline representative in Auckland reassured me they would send my baggage from Santiago to my house in California. It was old baggage. I no longer needed it, nor the things inside for this trip.

Thinking About Baggage Can Be Mentally Draining - Actually and Metaphorically.

I got home, and my baggage showed up a few days later. The airline, security, and customs had opened it, as evidenced by notes from the various inspection stations. Cool. Everything was there. For me, it was freeing not to worry about it any longer. I managed through my travels without it and traveled much lighter.

I could not help wondering if my baggage had a better experience than me.

Throughout my trip, I fought with what I carried and what I packed in my baggage. I pondered my experience and realized that occasionally, I was being held back by baggage. Or maybe it was the thought of not having it. While it turned out OK, I realized what this baggage issue was doing to me.

I Became a Victim of My Baggage - Actually and Metaphorically.

> "Our battered suitcases were piled on the sidewalk again; we had longer ways to go. But no matter, the road is life."
>
> – Jack Kerouac, On the Road (1958) from The Tao of Travel, Paul Theroux

TAKE AWAY: This chapter is about what slows us down. Misunderstanding the rules and expectations, incorrect assumptions, unpreparedness, and hanging on to problems too long. How we react (not great) or respond (better) to our baggage challenges helps us move forward. Recognizing, managing, and letting go of the baggage challenges that slow us down leads to increased speed, greater clarity, lighter burdens, and more authentic experiences—also, peace of mind.

PART II:
PONDERING

I'M A TRAVELING MAN; I'M A TRAVELERS' FAN

I'm a Traveling Man; I'm a Travelers' Fan
Travel starts before the plane, before the cruise, before the train.
Travel starts because of work, within a thought, a dream, or perk.
The travelers' path can be some fun, perhaps a blur or one of stun.
The stress is real, the pain renowned, and whether one could feel
     beat down.

We're tired, we're wired, we're perspired, and together sit in seats undesired.
We share the load, share the road, share the path but not the bath (except
     in Japan).
We've laughed, we've cried, we've feared, we've cheered.
We're happy, we're sad, we've griped, we're wiped.

Emotions high, we find all types; a great response could be some wipes.
I point the way, give a hug, buy a meal, share the plug.
We share the line, share the wine, share the pain when we deplane.
The babies cry, the people cough, and in the end, we all get off.

And on the seats, do we recline or pass and simply decline?
When the seat in front slides back, do we push back in our attack?
The armrest and screen shades, the cause of many wars,
Trying to sort out between what's mine and what's yours.

I've seen stranger things, to my surprise, but seek to see through
     strangers' eyes.

The talks and walks, the back and forth, the ups and downs, and
all ways North.
The guys and gals, the mates and friends. And those we may never
meet again.
And while we can't always stay, we should never forget the people along
the way.
We run, we wait, we sit, we're late. And such, my friend, is the traveler's fate.

MOM

Olympic Airways, Athens-Rhodes (Orthodox Easter weekend)

> "We shall not cease from exploration. And the end of all our exploring will be to arrive where we started and know the place for the first time."
>
> – T.S. Eliot, Little Gidding

My mother sat beside me on the flight from Athens to Rhodes, Greece. I dozed off. I was dreaming or having another past-life experience about riding a horse and being in a battle. I was a Greek warrior wearing a breast-plate, had bronze skin, was muscular (definitely not real), and had no fear. Unfortunately, a sword was thrust through me just as I admired myself. I fell from the horse with a thud when the plane slammed onto the runway, jarring me back to reality.

No doubt, a Greek pilot who was practicing short runway landings.

This would be my first trip to Greece since I left as a child, traveling with my mother and my oldest and youngest brothers. We arrived at Rhodes Airport with too much baggage. We met a relative with an undersized car and a friend with another car for the luggage. Over the years, my mother sent clothing and such to relatives, so most of what we brought would be given as gifts.

A 45-minute drive later, we found ourselves in the village where our mother was raised. We walked between new homes, and homes crumbled or crumbling. The older houses were similarly shaped: two rooms with an arch and curtain separating the two halves. The front room was the living space, while the back room was a common sleeping area. In the front, a built-in oven, a hole in the concrete where a fire was started, was on one wall. A small gas stove served to heat water for coffee or washing clothing. I remember the concrete was cold. There was one electrical outlet in each half of the house.

Around the village, we visited people who had been there all their lives. We ate Greek cookies and drank ouzo or coffee, or both. My brothers and I tried to piece together the conversation with the dozen or so Greek words we knew. The locals complimented our mother and her sons trailing her.

I like Rhodes. It is a big enough island to have things to do. It was interesting to see the Turkish influence on the island for hundreds of years during the Ottoman reign and then the Venetian Italians who occupied the island between World War I and II. It was like watching National Geographic in "living history" on the island.

My 23andMe confirmed the island genealogical maze. I am part of Southern Europe, Western Middle East, North Africa, and a little sub-Saharan from when people had no borders. They just migrated from place to place.

We drove through village after village - Lindos, Faliraki, Afandou and recalled these names that our father mentioned from having been stationed on Rhodes in the U.S. Coast Guard, maintaining the Voice of America during the start of the Cold War. The villages had large open squares and olive trees in the middle of each. Older men around a small round table sat on folding chairs, smoking unfiltered cigarettes and playing some version of tavli (backgammon) - leathery, wrinkled, worn, and proud. The backgammon boards were worn as well. Grooves were worn into the panels where the marble pieces were slid into and out of after years of play. Everything is the same from generations past.

The island of Rhodes also has a city with the same name. This was a little confusing, but no worse than New York, New York. The city of Rhodes was touristy, with the castle of the Knights of Saint John, cobblestone roads, shops, restaurants, and the entrance to the harbor where one of the Seven Wonders of the World, the Colossus of Rhodes, once stood. Three old Greek windmills and an old Greek church lined the harbor where my parents were married on Halloween. These windmills were also included in pictures my father had taken many years before. Most of what I saw was the same.

I grew up with three brothers and a sister. Additionally, one half-brother, much older than me, had joined the U.S. Air Force, and I didn't know him well. When he visited, he was a dick. Still is. My other half-brother didn't speak English, and I didn't speak Greek. I met him a couple of times after. Nice guy. He lives in Athens with his family.

We were like the Brady Bunch except from one family and just one sister, an average American family. I had wiry hair, a darker complexion, a unibrow, big ears, a somewhat deformed uvula (so I spoke nasally), and was clumsier than my siblings. I think most kids go through periods where they feel like they were the adopted kid in their family due to a DNA hoax, birth order, or some other general childhood trauma. I just grew up feeling different, generally not in a good way.

It was worse for my mother when her friends saw "the blonde, brown, and red-headed American family" crammed into the station wagon, including "the Greek kid." Then, they would ask my mother why she was taking "the Greek kid" with her. I learned somewhere that the locals considered themselves more from Rhodes than from Greece. Where was David Sedaris when I needed him?

Afterward, my family moved to Miami. Occasionally, my mother would take one or a few of us kids to the Greek Orthodox Church. We rode the bus for an hour each way. Somehow, my mother figured out how to navigate the transit system between the city and county bus networks. We took the bus to school, the doctor and dentist's offices, the fish market, and Sears, where we did the clothes shopping every August for school.

At the Greek Orthodox Church, my brothers and I fended for ourselves. Our mother shushed us while we coughed and choked at the incense. We watched the Greek parishioners make their change from the offering dish as it went by. We drank wine from the spoon the priest splashed into our mouths and ate bread. Greeks figured out how to make bread with the most crust. Maybe the Greeks invented bread, although Wikipedia says it was created 10,000 years earlier.

To pass the time, since the liturgy was spoken in Greek, I would count the colored window discs that surrounded the dome or stare endlessly at the myriad of mosaic windows that showed images of church history. One I remember the best is a soldier on a horse piercing someone on the ground (maybe that's where my previous vision came from). Once, I tried to make the deep chanting noise like the cantor. I wanted that job. My mother gave me a stern look when she heard me.

After, we made a beeline to the break room for a Krispy-Kreme donut. We didn't attend church often enough, and the bus ride was long, but we still had our imaginations.

Back in the village, everyone seemed somehow related. I didn't realize at first how many relatives I had. And it was wild how many people were still there decades later. Since the conversations exceeded the few Greek words I knew, and since I couldn't remember each relative, it seemed a good idea to start making a Greek family tree. So, I bought a spiral notebook, sat down for coffee with my mother, and asked who belonged to whom.

What I mistook for my mother's hesitancy of the English language I learned had more to do with who didn't belong to whom. I was at most two or three lines and boxes into the family tree when I realized there were too many lines or too few boxes. I used dashed lines where there were conflicting stories.

I asked some people we met if the lines and boxes were correct, which tended to end in an argument and more ouzo. My mother suggested making the tree or asking people about it might be a bad idea. I agreed.

At night, my two brothers and I slept in one bed - as adults. Fred took the middle position since he was the youngest.

Running water and electricity were introduced during many residents' lifetimes. A bus probably ran a couple of times a day through the village to the neighboring towns and then to the central city of Rhodes – still no emission controls. I wondered how my mother and her sister and brother fared as children. They just made it work. My mother often said someone would pick them up and drive them.

The stores around the city squares mainly had stayed the same for forty or more years. The butcher, my mother said, was the same family. Chickens, goats, lamb, and some pig legs were hanging, waiting to be purchased—not cooled nor frozen. It was not nicely packaged like we were used to seeing. Flies buzzing around. This was the real world.

We kept walking and visiting. From house to house, we saw pictures of my mother and our American father from many years earlier. We saw black-and-white photos of the village, soldiers, and relatives who had long passed on - some didn't quite fit the family tree book.

Even after many years of being gone, villagers questioned if I was part of this "American" family. As we visited one relative's house, the matron was excited to show me a picture of her "side" of the family, which I looked more like. It was like the app that shows what I would look like 20 years later. I was part of a branch that had forked a couple of generations previously and had died out.

I learned more about my background through relatives and stories, mismatched family lines, and 23andMe. Some of it made sense, and some is lost to history.

Rhodes was a robust shipping stop between the Middle East and Europe. While I wrote elsewhere about the King of Italy visiting Rhodes, his entourage and many Italians undoubtedly came. This was a part of my mother's story.

Another part was about a princess of Iraq in Rhodes. My grandmother was a housekeeper and tended to an Iraqi family. My mother, then a young girl, stayed with this family. The story was about an Iraqi princess who visited Rhodes, met, and married a Greek man, which was frowned upon. They escaped to Athens. A car wreck around a cliff later, he went missing, and she was sent back to Iraq.

With Rhodes at this Mediterranean crossroads, it made sense that people from so many countries would have passed through.

I will probably not understand DNA and my relatives enough in this lifetime, but I found missing links. Like the son in Big Fish, he sought to separate fact from fiction in his father's life. For me, it was my mother. And, in most cases, her stories lined up.

Over the years, these stories were not so different from those who claimed to have invented certain technologies, met celebrities, and accomplished outlandish feats. These stories make us human in one sense; in another, they stretch us to think further.

TAKE AWAY: In a recent Forbes article on aging, the author wrote that the success rate for start-ups is directly related to age, which is related to experience[1]. In my innovation management work, we intentionally brought in an outsider to give an experiential perspective, alternatives to many of the 'same' solutions, and considerations for other constituents. Experience matters, or companies may be forced to relive failures from the past.

---

[1] https://www.forbes.com/sites/kmehta/2022/08/23/older-entrepreneurs-outperform-younger-foundersshattering-ageism

ARNIE

JetBlue, Boston–Long Beach

An exhausting week on the road.

A last-minute flight back home.

Rushing to Boston Airport.

A long security line.

A long line to board.

Stow my luggage overhead.

Keep my laptop bag.

A window seat.

A lot of work to do.

A six-and-a-half-hour flight.

An empty middle seat next to me.

Score!

I closed my eyes for a moment. A sigh of arrival. The smell of the airplane. Leather seats. The passengers quieted as the last bags were loaded overhead. Flight attendants walked the aisles, directing, helping, and saying hello. I stretched my legs and body. I had a lot of work to do.

And then, just as the door closed, a flight attendant with two kids in tow slid through. The little girl took the middle seat in the row ahead of me.

The little boy sat in the middle seat next to me.

The little boy clutched a pack of 32 sticks of gum and had a wad in his mouth.

He was well dressed—wearing a pair of slacks, a pressed shirt, leather shoes, and a sports coat. Neatly combed hair. A gentleman. He seemed content, his feet dangling. He buckled his seatbelt and checked out the video screen. His older sister turned around to make sure he was okay.

Another stick of gum was unwrapped and in his mouth.

He told me his name was Arnie, he was six, and he would visit his grandparents. He had flown across the country "lots of times and knew what to do." SpongeBob came on the screen, and another stick of gum went in.

I suspect he was the child of airline employees, traveling "standby" and boarded when all the paying passengers were seated. As a former airline employee, I understood the process.

I remember the emotional pain I felt the first time I watched my son (probably eight) and daughter (probably six) walk down the jet bridge without their mother or me, traveling to Cleveland to visit their grandparents. My son in a nice outfit, my daughter in a dress just went. Both had flown more airline miles than most people have in their lifetimes, including a few international trips and assured me they "knew what to do" as they left me waiting at the gate. My heart broke, and I cried, wondering how this separation would affect them for the rest of their lives without someone they knew nearby.

Several years later, I relived my pain. As my son traveled alone still as a child, no one met him at the gate. Flights changed; communications were mixed up. A flight attendant brought him home.

As the jet bridge pulled away from the plane, I felt Arnie tap my arm, and he asked if we could switch seats. He said he didn't like the middle seat. His feet were dangling and swinging back and forth.

"How about if you sit by the window during take-off and landing, and I'll sit by the window during the rest of the flight so I can do my work? Okay?"

"Okay. Thank you, sir."

We switched seats. Ernie propped himself up with his little fingers holding onto the bottom of the windowsill so he could see outside better. I fell asleep.

Some people don't talk. Some talk too much—or talk too loudly. Some take up too much space. Some smell bad or wear too much perfume or not enough. Some commandeer the armrest (protocol says that the person in the middle seat should have both armrests in the down position. The captain of a recent American Airlines flight also included this in a moving preflight announcement).

Some people are happy, some sad, most mind their own business, and some not.

I've generally had good experiences with others while traveling. I've sat by millionaires, actors, CEOs of large companies, a guy who had a heart attack, youngsters and older people, people from all around the world, scared people, drunk people, coworkers, and customers (two rules not to do).

I awoke over Buffalo, and Arnie was still sitting, looking out the window. I noticed his pack of gum was missing a few more sticks.

We swapped back to our assigned seats, and I cracked open my laptop to work.

The flight attendant came by, offering headphones, drinks, and food. She asked if he wanted anything. He said he'd like a headset and a Sprite. I handed my credit card to the flight attendant to pay for it. I would have appreciated someone doing that for my son and daughter, although we generally packed them snacks. And, back then, food was even commonplace on planes.

Some people who had never met previously have plane affairs for the couple of hours they are together, never intending to see each other again. Chance meetings. Deals struck. Stories swapped. Memories made.

I love to travel because we meet people we would not otherwise get to meet—the Universe's meet-people lottery. It is an opportunity to experience someone else's life for a few hours—good or bad, long or short, happy or sad. Some experiences we take, others we give. If I had a nickel for every time I sat by someone with a relationship problem, I could afford First Class.

We were over Denver. Arnie was humming the Dora song. In went another stick of gum. He asked me if we were getting ready to land so he could relieve me of sitting by the window. He unwrapped a piece of gum and held it in his six-year-old fingers for me. I gladly accepted the gum and dodged the middle seat.

I remember traveling with my son and daughter to Europe—sometimes for work, other times to take a long weekend break. My son first flew when he was three or four—to Japan. As he got older, he would disappear on the flight, hanging out with flight attendants, asking questions, and probably helping. "Hey, Dad," one flight he said, "that flight attendant is pouring the wine wrong."

Sometimes, we meet our seatmate late in the trip, only to wish we had started the conversation earlier. Excited people, weary people. Soldiers on their way overseas or on their way home. A newlywed couple or a family.

Somewhere over Arizona, the plane began to descend into Long Beach. By now, it was dark, and Arnie was ready to sit by the window again, his legs twitching. He was still chewing but had long run out of fresh gum. We switched seats. All I saw was the back of his head as he looked out the window. He was excited, wearing his little suit, tie, and leather shoes, getting ready to see his grandparents.

The flight attendant came by, embarrassed that I paid for his headset and Sprite since it should have been complimentary. It was worth it.

We landed, and the flight attendant took him and his sister to meet his grandparents.

I think of Arnie and what a lovely boy he was. So well-behaved. His sister turned around to check on him from time to time. While Arnie talked to me through all the gum he was chewing, I caught most of it.

I never once felt like I wouldn't treat him as I would my own.

Walking behind them, the flight attendant handed Arnie and his sister to their grandparents.

Arnie turned around, waved, and said, "Thank You."

Just like my son would do.

Just like the gentleman he was.

And then I thought, what happened to all of that gum?

TAKE AWAY: Listen

PEOPLE YOU MEET ALONG THE WAY

ValueJet, Dallas–Atlanta - Newark

Jack Kornfield tells the story of a lady changing flights at an airport. She stopped to get a bottle of water and some cookies at the minimart in the airport terminal, then sat at one of the random waiting tables. Soon, a man asked to sit across from her. She said, "Okay." Out of the corner of her eye, she saw the man open the bag of cookies, and he offered her one. Confused, she accepted it. A few minutes later, when he offered her another, she became annoyed that he was eating her cookies. She took it with shock. They called her flight, and she walked to her gate. On arrival, she reached into her bag to get her boarding pass and found her unopened bag of cookies. In shock, she realized that the cookies the man offered her at the table were not hers but his.

As we travel, we meet people wherever we are and wherever they are. We let them know they mean something to us, and sometimes they let us know we made a difference to them—and they are all around us. Travel is one of those experiences where all forms and levels of lifestyles commingle. Air, train, ship, ferry—it doesn't matter.

When traveling, I look for people waiting to be found. Is there an experience waiting to happen?

On my 25th trip (or so) to Canada to speak at a customer conference, the border patrol agent asked why I was coming to Canada.

"I am speaking at a conference."

"Do you have an I.D. or something that says what kind of speaking you do?"

I pulled out a business card. James Menge, Technology Evangelist.

"What church are you with?" he asked.

"No church," I replied.

"Your card says Evangelist," he inquired.

"No church," I replied.

The other time I screwed up with an immigration person was in Nassau, where the officer wore Z-Coil spring shoes. I said, "Cool shoes." He walked me over to another immigration officer who took his time leafing page by page through my passport, causing me to nearly miss my flight.

Back to Canada. Not a believer, the immigration agent walked me to a little room to talk with the Immigration Director. Same scenario - about bringing religion into Canada. What did I study? Theology. What work did I do abroad? Missionary.

"What was the problem?" I asked.

After a cursory look in my briefcase, they found a book given to me by some rogue Canadian employees, "How to Be Canadian," and a "Canada Kicks Ass" T-shirt. A few minutes later, some folks coming to the conference saw me in the little room and asked if I was in trouble. They were Canadian and vouched that I was not there to preach a religion, although I was working on my book, Business Evangelism.

People worldwide have stories, something to teach, something for us to learn if we listen. Stories and customs are fun. A customer in Brazil shared that sometimes people must suffer before moving ahead. In Ecuador, of the equator, the people are proud to be "the keepers of the line." In France, food is a social experience as much or more as nourishment. In Japan, people are thoughtful of personal space, even nearby.

I like flying to the Caribbean and South America, where people still clap when the plane lands. I'm unsure if they're glad the pilot got us there, that the plane made it, happy to be where we're going, or just happy not to be where they were. They would undoubtedly have a story to tell even if it were a perfect flight.

Traveling almost anywhere in Africa, the people enriched my expression of life. On my first flight to Africa, I traveled with a friend to Kenya. Way in the back of the plane, on an overnight flight from London, we were greeted, hugged, and became part of the passenger family - little sleep, lots of laughter. Shared food. Happiness. That never happens in Business Class.

In Europe, many capitals have flights from African countries linked to their past. In London, it is Kenya, Tanzania, and South Africa. In France, you find French-speaking people from Morocco (Maroc, which is why the three-letter World Cup code for Morocco is MAR), Mali, Niger, Nigeria, and Ivory Coast. In Lisbon, it's Angola and Mozambique. In Frankfurt, it would be Namibia.

Most countries from South America have roots in Spain, except for Brazil (Portugal) and Argentina, which also has roots in Italy. It is always funny to hear people say, "Learn Spanish, and you can speak Portuguese and Italian" (or learn any of the three to speak the others). Having worked in Brazil for a year, my limited Spanish only got me into trouble. I learned critical phrases from the Taco Bell chihuahua commercials.

I remember telling a friend traveling to Japan, who was worried about not being able to read Japanese, that most of the signs are in English and not to worry about getting around. Having lived there for six years, the Japanese signs must have started looking like English because she told me nothing was in English the next time I saw her.

Korea reinvented itself in the 1980s when I was there in the military. The 1988 Olympics made Korea the significant economic engine it is today.

Korea has moved on and is now one of the world's leading cosmetics-producing countries, music capitals (K-pop), and television (Squid Game) game show producers.

China was a mystery. In a short time, it modernized and became a world superpower. The people were always friendly, caring, and efficient, even if all we spoke was a form of sign language. On one of my first trips to China, my son and I took the overnight train from Shanghai to Beijing. Steaming hot water at each end of the train car was ample to heat the dried noodle soup for a meal.

After a day of visiting Beijing, my son and I took a two-night train to Tibet. He asked if a flight existed, but I wanted to take my time. The train was the most contemplative way to travel to Lhasa. As we approached Lhasa, I finished reading The Old Patagonian Express by Paul Theroux about his train trip from Boston to Mendoza in Argentina.

Getting somewhere should set the stage for where you're going. Flying to Orlando and Las Vegas, take Southwest. Traveling to Tibet, take the train. Taking the leading airline of most countries gives you a taste of what to expect. Flying Ryanair and Spirit Airlines show the most essential elements of being human. The "getting there" is as important as the "being there."

In Russia, the people were friendly and open. The food was excellent. I made sure to visit the Moscow Yaroslavsky Train Station so I would know where, in the future, to board the Trans-Siberian Express. I'm not sure why anyone thinks 14 days on a train is an "express!"

I met great people in each country on trains, buses, and a ferry from Tallin to Helsinki. At each stop, as I got further from Western Europe, what was familiar was becoming less and less. But, more and more, people showed me what to eat, where to go, what to see.

A fellow traveler spends the end of each year in India at an ashram. Another seatmate had just returned from the same Spanish pilgrimage I had walked several years earlier. I spent six hours on a trans-continental flight next to a psychologist on Oprah and a 45-minute commuter flight next to a female adult star (unknown to me). One flight was too long, and the other needed to be longer.

I learn from my seatmates. I was upgraded to First Class on a reconnection, roughly a $10,000 ticket. Sitting next to me was one of the senior people from an expensive finance consulting company. He hated everything about travel: this airline, First Class, and the country we were going to.

"If this is as good as it gets, I'd rather stay home," he said.

I agreed; he should have stayed home.

People can sense and know our passion. An audience member emailed me a picture he created of me in a priestly robe—it was when I started calling myself an evangelist. He changed how I viewed myself. In traveling, and when the conversation permits, I ask executives what they look for most in staff. Dedication and lower costs tend to be the main answer. Once in a while, I get to hear about transcendence – an employee who makes a difference.

While I generally avoid traveling with my boss or anyone up line, occasionally, it can't be helped. Working at the fringe of most companies, I found myself in trouble more often than I wanted. On the last day of my job at the company where I spent most of my career, I sat next to my boss on the way back from a customer meeting. He was a guy who gave me more chances than I remember. I cried.

While the truth is that not everyone treats us well, some people change our lives for good.

On another flight, I sat next to a customer for three hours and heard everything wrong with my company's product, service, and people. Later, he would renew his contract with us. Even after I left my company, I visited this man, helped him with his business, met the Board, and ate with his children. He trusted me, our product, and then our people.

I learned to model success after this man, not so much in what he did but in how he viewed what I did.

A dozen trips and a few short years later, I attended his funeral.

Some people you leave, and some never leave you.

TAKE AWAY: Everybody matters.

MANCATION

American Airlines, Dallas-London
British Airways, London-Nairobi
British Airways, Nairobi-London
Aer Lingus, Dublin-London

Men in their twenties flock to Cancun for Spring Break.

Thirty-something men get together in Las Vegas for the Final Four basketball tournament.

Forty-somethings tend to hang with friends at a bar or barbecue.

Fifty and sixty-somethings take spouse trips and spend time together on the side.

Men take golf trips and motorcycle rides, go fishing and sailing, discover other lands like North America and Antarctica, or sail around the world. Men travel differently when they're with other men than with their families.

Not to be outdone, women generally, too, travel differently when with other women. Spacation. Shopcation. More time by the pool. A cabana. Margaritas. Less time doing, more time being, and more time enjoying.

And neither of these is 100%.

While at the Hotel Nacional Bar in Havana, discussing an upcoming trip to Kenya, my wife and I met a tall, thin English writer for the BBC. He described all the places that English people travel to. Historically, the English are the most traveled people in the world, although I read recently that the younger

English are losing their sense of geography. We discussed why most Americans would not survive abroad - something to do with bathrooms, sinks, smells, food, tiny hotel rooms, lack of personal space, language, customs, and not ordering latte in the afternoon in Italy.

The BBC guy also told us what we would see on safari since my wife, and I had plans to go in eight weeks. For an hour, he described the Serengeti, the plains, the trees, the animals, and his favorite part, the lion hunt, the kill, and the near-dying prey's bones cracking while still breathing. Listening to an Englishman talk about travel was like watching National Geographic in real time. My wife was out.

A week later, the husband of a friend of my wife, maybe she just wanted him out of the house for 12 days, volunteered to go.

Mancation. Most men, in general, go with the flow.

Here was the conversation:

Me: "Hey, Randy, meet the British Airways flight for Nairobi at London Heathrow on May 15th at 11 p.m. Visit your doctor to get shots. I'll email you the tour conductor's address so you can send a check. Anything else you want to do?"

Randy: "Yeah, when we return to London, I'd love to visit the Hooters in Nottingham, then drive through Liverpool to Edinburgh, drink scotch, fly to Ireland, drink whiskey, drive for a day, fly back to London, and then go home."

Me: "Cool. Done. Let's throw in the William Wallace monument. See you in London."

Click.

I had never traveled with Randy and did not know much about him.

Six weeks later, Randy and I met in London, caught our overnight flight to Nairobi, and sat with a Kenyan lady between us who told us what to eat, what to expect, and how to stay safe. We slept a few hours and landed, staring at a giraffe next to the runway. With our baggage in tow, we met up with the tour group and headed for the first stop of our safari.

Randy had packed several bottles of liquor for our trip. For hours, we traveled on what would be like an unpaved interstate pothole with an occasional flat strip of median, listening to the liquor bottles clanging. To get rid of the noise, we started drinking. Problem solved.

Our mancation went well. We slept in lodges and tents, ate fresh food, breathed clean air, drove a lot, and were as close to wild animals as possible without becoming food.

We ran across the occasional lion and leopard, teaching their young how to hunt and eat. A crack and crunch into the wildebeest's leg or rib cage was all we heard. There was a lot of blood, a mess just like the English guy at the bar said it would be. Someone cheekily hummed "The Circle of Life" from The Lion King.

On the last day in Kenya, Randy wanted to run through the fields near the camp; I wanted to climb a tree and get a picture. Both were bad ideas and certainly only likely to have been suggested by our families if they wanted to eliminate us. We paid our driver to drive us into the wild, did our man things, and returned to camp.

We flew back to London, rented a car, and drove on the other side of the road than we were used to. We asked someone for directions to Edinburgh and were told it would take us two days. Right. Two American guys. He was more concerned with being sure we would drive on the left side.

We arrived at Hooters in Nottingham at 9 a.m. It wasn't open (shocker), so we waited for them to open. Chicken wings for breakfast were good. At the time, it was the only Hooters outside of North America. We were the only people there for the first two hours. We ate our wings, took a selfie, and got back on the road.

The drive was surreal. We passed the Roman Wall (as far north as the Roman Empire stretched) and stopped to see the William Wallace Monument (he didn't look like Mel Gibson, but he was a hero nonetheless). We saw a white castle, not the White Castle restaurant, but a literal White Castle. We arrived at our hotel at night and felt satisfied that in 24 hours, we were on two continents and just drove the length of Great Britain.

We talked. We didn't talk. No requirement. No guilt. Randy did his thing. I did mine. No pressure.

Whiskey is a religion. People have strong opinions about whiskey. It could be a taste, knowledge, experience, and comfort: the Scottish Whiskey Experience, Glenfiddich Distillery, Glenlivet Distillery, Macallan. We didn't get to the other 130 distilleries and still need to make more trips.

We flew west across the Irish Sea to Belfast instead of taking the ferry. Flights seemed more convenient, plus we had to return the car and pick another one up in Ireland. Some European airlines took low cost a step further than we did in the U.S.-charging for luggage, restricting carry-on luggage to be the size of a notepad, charging for drinks and food, and 4:00 a.m. flights seemed the norm. This has become the norm worldwide.

The 4 a.m. flight is like taking the night train - a very different set of bleary-eyed travelers than during the day and evening, except to or from Las Vegas. The places looked different. Airport shops were closed. No restaurants. No talking. The rules were different. Men seem to drag themselves like a sack of potatoes. That's how we went—like a sack of potatoes.

We gathered our baggage a flight later and grabbed a rental car ("car hire"). The drive from Belfast to Dublin was lined with castles, and we stopped at villages for coffee and tea breaks.

As attractive as the villages and stopovers were, we also came across several places related to the paranormal, pre-history, and burial tombs like the Tombs of Newgrange, predating the pyramids, one of the oldest and largest Neolithic burial chambers in Europe. Monasterboice (burial ground), Ballynoe (stone circle and 100+ kings), and the Hill of Tara (1,500 years old) were worth stopping at, even to capture a sense of the place. Years later, I still have dreams of visiting here.

We made it to Dublin, visited the Guinness Brewery, and found a place to sleep for a few hours before our 4:30 a.m. flight back to London and home.

Mancations take different forms, and depending on the person you are traveling with, they have different outcomes.

On a different, more recent trip to London, I went with a well-traveled colleague (50+ cruises). Less of a mancation and more of a workation, we found a couple of days to meander. Maybe that's what men do… meander. While we did not always plan a pathway, we had endpoints in mind. So, we wandered through London for two days—20,000 steps each day. The boat from Greenwich (yes, I straddled the line where time starts North and South) to Westminster gave a different perspective to a city I had visited a hundred times.

In India, the Taj Mahal view that most tourists photograph is the backside. The front is the side facing the river Yumana. So it is with many of the buildings in London. Cruising under London Bridge (less scenic) and the Tower Bridge (more scenic) and stopping along the waterway were iconic. (I sound like a tourist guide). My takeaway was that only one generation ago, the river would have been the usual way to travel.

I enjoy taking coworkers, colleagues, and friends off the beaten path. Prague to Berlin on the train, London to Paris on the Eurostar, and Shanghai to Beijing on the high-speed rail are each an itinerary that most would fly between. I appreciated the awakening of co-travelers who trusted me and ventured off the beaten path.

Never travel in a straight line.

TAKE AWAY: This chapter discusses our interactions with people, places, and experiences. Perspective is essential as we consider options, obstacles, and opportunities.

CAT'S IN THE CRADLE

American Airlines, Miami Melbourne (Florida)

Half of the passengers bound for Melbourne, Florida, moved toward the gate when the gate agent asked for anyone who needed special assistance. Ten, twenty, thirty, forty wheelchairs went into the jet bridge. No exaggeration. I was going to visit my father. Anything past the first row would result in a delay in getting off. I felt it. I saw it.

Knowing this, I sat in the front of the plane and got off before most people. I was visiting my father for the last time while he was alive.

I remember many of my life transitions as though they were chapters in a book. In his book Life is in the Transitions, Bruce Feiler writes about the non-linear life. *"We can't ignore these central times of life; we can't wish or will them away. We have to accept them, name them, mark them, share them, and eventually convert them into a new and vital fuel for remaking our life stories."*

Before I was 18, I felt I already had two or three life changes. At 18, I had another when I joined the Air Force and moved to Japan. Again, when I got married, when my son was born, and then again when my daughter was born. My life changed again when I was going to visit my father.

As a child, I wrote on paper to anyone who would write back. I wrote to airlines worldwide for schedules and pictures of their planes. I even got a response from the Cuban airline in 1970, much to the displeasure of one of my father's Coast Guard buddies who swore the CIA would somehow relate him to me. I wrote to cousins, my grandmother in New York, and her perennial bachelor brother, Uncle Joe.

Uncle Joe sent me comics and puzzles from the Sunday New York Times. He rolled them up tight, cut off the ends of an envelope, and inserted the rolled clippings. I read the comics each week while my father worked on the crossword puzzle that Uncle Joe included. Invariably, there would also be an article I didn't understand that my father could relate to, generally about New York or politics.

Periodically, my father took my younger brothers and me to the local library. At the time, it was housed in a stone building. The children's books were in a sizeable stepdown circular at one end of the building, with books surrounding the perimeter. I felt as though I could live there. At one point in my life, I had 40 boxes of books in my private library.

Growing up, time with my father consisted of my younger brothers and me working with him at the apartment building and empty lot he and my mother owned in an old part of Miami. We pulled weeds, refurbished apartments, fixed sinks, replaced toilets, rewired bare electrical wires from the 1920s, cut sheet rock, built walls, filled holes, and painted. We were introduced to Hank Williams, Freddy Fender, Willie Nelson (who I'd fly with later in life from Los Angeles to Austin), Charley Pride (who I'd fly with later in life from Dallas to London), and Dolly Parton (who I'd take selfies with wherever I found her mural painted) on the AM radio, WWOK—no Walkman. No iPod. No iPhone. No EarPods. No earplugs.

Dad was a heavy smoker and, at the time, had both lungs. While working with him, he went into coughing convulsions. He coughed up blood, then lit up another cigarette. At 13 years old, I wondered how I would get him to a hospital. Willie Nelson sang. The life lesson was imprinted.

While in the Air Force, I wrote on paper to my father and grandmother, his mother. My father wrote with a 1950s style of all-caps architectural font and perfect penmanship. My grandmother had a more scripted writing style.

They'd write back faithfully. I felt happy they wrote back, although I'm unsure what we wrote about. Just before she died, my grandmother told me my penmanship was terrible.

I would visit my father for marriage, work, children, and something about politics. I appreciated his perspective. Earlier in life, as an older teenager, I would meet up with my father at a local bar hangout in Miami. We each downed a beer and talked.

My dad was a crusty, old-school sort of man's man. He lied about his age to join the Navy as a sailor in World War II. That's what boys did to fight in a war. Years later, he retired from the Coast Guard. He was a mechanic and worked in the engine room on ships. During World War II, he fought in the Pacific and traveled through the Panama Canal in one of the then-largest ships. He served on board the vessel that powered the Voice of America broadcasting into the Southern Soviet Union and Eastern Europe during the Cold War, still one of the most powerful radio transmitters. My father was rugged and built things with his hands out of seemingly nothing. He was tough, swore, drank a six-pack of beer every night, claimed a beer gut, and chain-smoked like the next cigarette was his last.

At this point, unfortunately, it was.

Later in life, my father became a friend. I trusted him. We discussed his pain as his marriage to my mother dissolved years before. We spoke of what being happy meant. We talked about love and commitment.

Not too many years later, my stepmother called to tell me that my father had emphysema. He had one lung removed a few years earlier. But one lung didn't stop him from smoking. He was going to die happy, not deprived, he said. She told me my father only had a couple of months to live.

I visited him several times over the next couple of months, always noticing and walking past the wheelchairs at the airport. I walked him to the bathroom when he couldn't go by himself. I gave him a sponge bath. I sat on the bed next to him, and we talked. I read to him. I lit a cigarette when he couldn't light the match himself. He said he was not a fan of lighters. We cried, and I held him. He didn't seem afraid, just steady.

My stepmother called one January morning to tell me my father had passed that night. He lived on a golf course. I was golfing. She told me to finish my round. It was sunny. I did.

I was glad I could spend the last few months with my father. While some memories stayed the same, I also learned new things. I realized my father had changed. Even after he passed away, I continued to learn about him from old pictures, slides, military travel records, papers he wrote, talking with my brothers, and recollections of our discussions.

As I travel, I find myself visiting the places he had been earlier. I walked on the pier where he was stationed when I was born. I saw the harbor he was stationed in at Rhodes. I saw a U.S. Coast Guard ship parked in the port in Malta. My brother Fred and I visited the Panama Canal, where he traveled through. My son and I visited islands around the South Pacific that he no doubt passed or stopped at.

At some point, I realized I inherited some of my father's inclinations, just as my brothers had.

I write. I included my father's published poem, Gullible's Travels, at the end of this book. While he writes about television advertising, the same would be true today of Internet ads and the many unnecessary purchases that regularly appear at my front door.

I swear.

I have a beer.

I travel.

I realized that my father not being perfect didn't matter.

I was old enough to know that I wasn't either.

American Airlines, Nassau – Miami – Dallas – Los Angeles

And he walked away, but his smile never dimmed,
He said, "I'm gonna be like him, yeah.
You know I'm gonna be like him."

—Harry Chapin, "The Cats in the Cradle"

And so, years later, my mind replays my time with my father.

Having spent a fair period of my life working in the airline industry, I learned what flying standby meant. It meant waiting for an empty seat on a plane. Early morning. Late night. One, two, or three days of waiting. That's how it went when I started traveling as an adult.

Even later, standby as a regular traveler became a thing. Or trying to take an earlier flight than the one I had a ticket for. Or it meant taking a later flight if I missed the one I was supposed to be on. Or it meant waiting to see if I would receive a seat upgrade.

During this standby period of my life, I learned tricks about which flights would have more available seats, switching airports at the last minute, taking a bus from Vancouver to Seattle because more seats were available or because I could spend more time in Vancouver and take the "red eye" flight home from Seattle. If the Paris flights were sold out, my kids and I would switch to London, Frankfurt, or Zurich. I paid little attention to how much my two children learned that flying was like changing lanes on the Interstate.

While traveling home to Southern California from Nassau, I needed to work late before leaving and arrive home early the following day. There would be no overnight option since red-eye flights travel east, and I was going west. The shortest option was a late flight to Dallas, overnight at the airport hotel for 4 hours, then the first flight home. During this period, wildfires were burning around my house, making me even more anxious to return. I mentioned this to my son (who lived in Dallas then) but told him I would sleep at the DFW airport hotel for a few hours.

My son was taking a late-night flight back to Dallas from Tampa the same night, and we decided to meet at the airport in Dallas for a few minutes. I got to the airport in Nassau and collected my three boarding passes (to Miami, Dallas, and Orange County). I wondered why one was in First Class and boarded my flight to Miami.

My flight arrived early in Miami, and I could see that the last flight west (to Los Angeles) had yet to depart. I ran to the gate and begged (Road Warriors do what we must do to get on a plane) the gate agent to let me board so I could get home to what was left of our neighborhood. The first gate agent said no, so I tried the next gate agent (Road Warriors keep trying until the plane leaves the gate). The second gate agent said yes.

I arrived in Los Angeles and turned on my cell phone, which started beeping, alerting me that someone was sending me urgent messages. My heart raced, thinking that something terrible had happened to my home. I saw three texts:

The first, from my son, said, "WHERE ARE YOU??!!"

The second, also from my son, said, "I HATE YOU."

The third, also from my son, said, "@MIA W8NG 4U SO WE CUD FLY2 DFW 2GETHR. SURPRISE!"

What made my son think that he could change his flights around like that on a whim?

Then I realized changing flights was something we did on a whim regularly. I realized my son had taken on my 'last-minute flight change' habit.

We share other traits: impatience, anger, caring, giving, laughing, and frustration at the same funny travel situations; we had empathy for passengers repacking bags at the check-in counters, overworked employees, flight crews still working past retirement age, finding ways to spend more time at an airport, and not traveling in a straight line.

A couple of years later, my son came to visit me. I dropped him off at the airport at 4:25 p.m. for a 5:35 p.m. flight. Ten minutes later, at 4:35, without missing a beat, he called from the jet bridge to say that he had successfully boarded an earlier flight and was now boarding.

His scheduled flight would turn out to be four hours late.

Who the heck does he think he is?

TAKE AWAY: As we develop our career, family, and sense of self, legacy becomes more prevalent. I learned how to be from those with more experience, and I met people who fashioned principles from things I did or said. The key is to be aware of each and celebrate both.

I'M NOT YOUR WIFE

American Airlines, Dallas–Anchorage
Alaska Airlines, Anchorage–Fairbanks - Barrow

"My frequent flier miles expire this year. How far can we go?"

– My brother, Fred.

I've had mixed experiences traveling with people for business or personal reasons. I've had not so great and great experiences traveling with first-time fliers and those who have flown more than I have. Each brings their perspective of how things should be or should not be, what "personal space" means, and how much they can drink and talk.

Again, in Up in the Air, Ryan Bingham (George Clooney) says to a colleague at airport security, "Never get behind people traveling with infants. I've never seen a stroller collapse in less than 20 minutes. Old people are worse. Their bodies are littered with hidden metal, and they never seem to appreciate how little time they have left. Bingo, Asians. They pack light, travel efficiently, and have a thing for slip-on shoes. Gotta love 'em."

One of my favorite co-travelers is Fred, my youngest brother. He asked me the question at the beginning of this chapter one summer. The answer was easy once I figured out how many miles he had. I use frequent flyer points on more obtuse routings and go-to destinations that the regular airline doesn't fly to. Generally, frequent flyer and hotel points are best used for trips out of the way, extravagant, frivolous, and even whimsical. We went through the pain of earning the points; why not enjoy them on the other end?

A month later, Fred and I met in Dallas for our 7,500-mile trip to Barrow, Alaska, 1,122 miles south of the North Pole, the furthest city we could fly on his frequent flyer points. That was what he asked, "How far can we go?"

This trip reminds me of another off-the-map experience that Fred and I had traveling to the Dry Tortugas, a set of islands seventy miles west of Key West. Having grown up in Miami, we never made the drive to Key West together. So, on another trip to Miami, we decided to explore and drive south.

Henry Flagler built the original route between Miami and Key West as a train line in the 1910s. This was when rich money was spent on projects that might not have made sense but were monumental. It's like the billionaire space flight industry today.

We drove through Homestead, where my family shopped at the Air Force base. At the time, it bordered the Everglades and was mainly an orange grove. As a kid, it seemed like it was in another state. It is still very different than Miami, thirty miles north.

From there, we drove from island to island, drank coffee, ate sunflower seeds, and stopped at some old rail bridges where people fish. We passed over the seven-mile bridge. We stopped at a few places where movie scenes from Meet the Fockers and some James Bond movies were filmed. I think one movie was an Arnold Schwarzenegger movie.

We got to Key West, checked into our lime-green B&B, and drank some beers at Sloppy Joe's, where Ernest Hemingway hung out. There were lots of picket fences and cats.

The next day, we explored more of Key West. Key West was only accessible by boat for the first 100 years of being a city until the rail line connecting to Miami was built between 1904 and 1912. Pan American Airways started in Key West in 1927 with a flight to Havana. A hurricane wiped out the rail line in 1935, and the Overseas Highway replaced it in 1938. We visited the end of the line train station.

On a whim, we took a float plane to the Dry Tortugas National Park. The Dry Tortugas started as a coal refueling point between New Orleans and Miami and afterward as a Union Civil War prison. Dr. Samuel Mudd was interred (he was sentenced for setting the leg of John Wilkes Booth, the assassin of Abraham Lincoln). Walking around the island, we felt as though we had stepped back a hundred years since we were "so far" from civilization, and nothing had changed on the island since the Civil War.

While the train line and the highway are the furthest that people typically travel to, the Dry Tortugas is the last bit of land in the U.S. It was "as far as we could go" on that trip.

Never travel in a straight line. Keep going.

Back to Dallas. We boarded our seven-hour flight to Anchorage. We talked about where we were in our lives, his work, my work, our kids getting older, what colleges they were in, and what they were studying. We talked about where we would go and what we would see in Alaska.

Just then, the plane pulled away from the gate and headed to the runway.

I thought Fred would spring the "peanut game" on me - a game he played with his kids as they traveled on multi-leg, all-day trips on Southwest Airlines - to see who could hold a peanut in their mouth the longest. He told me about this when we met in New York in June 2001, three months before 9/11.

We arrived in Anchorage late evening and stayed at the airport hotel. We met a seemingly angry woman who told us she was Greek. Was she angry before or after we told her we were Greek? She started telling us about how terrible Greek men are. She began with uncaring, unfaithful, unorthodox, unaware, and under-appreciating. We told her we were half-Greek and didn't know any Greek men. We had an early flight, so she gave us our room key, and we slept uncomfortably for a few hours wondering if she would stab us in the middle of the night.

The following day, back to the airport, check-in, boarding passes, front of the passenger section, window and aisle, bulkhead. Some travelers have religion about the bulkhead. The leading benefits include no one reclining in front of them, a place to put their feet sans shoes on the wall since that's what they do at home, and non-raising armrests to be sure others don't thigh-creep.

We boarded from the back of the plane. Fred was excited since there were no seats between us and the cockpit, like in First Class. Except that there was a 40-foot cargo section between us and the cockpit. As the "cockpit" door opened, we saw open air. We were told we could only bring in checked luggage and only the amount of alcohol that we could consume in the time we were there.

Airplane seat configurations are funny. On an Olympic Airways Boeing 747 flight from Athens, Greece, to New York, Fred and I sat in the non-smoking row. It was right across the emergency door aisle from the flight attendants sitting backward. The no-smoking light went off after the plane took off, and the flight attendants lit their cigarettes. Fred asked about the non-smoking section since that is where we were seated. One of the flight attendants pulled out a sheet of paper, thought about it, and said, "Yes, you both are the two non-smoker seats."

Having been in the Air Force, I knew that Barrow was interesting because it was the endpoint of the 1950s DEW (Defense Early Warning) system stretching across the Arctic Circle to warn the U.S. of an incoming Russian missile attack. The perforated steel planking laid down for the temporary-be-came-permanent runway, a few rundown buildings here and there, and a few research buildings are still in use.

Barrow, a city still mainly of indigenous people, was mostly pickup trucks, unpaved roads, and a grocery store. Even in early September, when we went, it was dark much of the day. The "furthest northern Mexican restaurant" was decent. Something Italian was also there. We took a local tour in a pickup, skipped the polar plunge (no change of clothes), and opted for the photo under the Arctic Whale Bone Arch.

Sibling travel is another dynamic in the world of travel. As kids, seven of us traveled in the Pontiac station wagon from Miami to New York during the summer—no air conditioning. Dad smoked. No singing. No video. No cell phone. No breaks. No seatbelts. No earplugs, again. My dad, Fred, and mom were upfront. Fred caught most of the second-hand smoke. Older brother and sister in the middle. At the back of the station wagon was the seat where Bob, my other younger brother, and I sat, facing backward. I'm convinced that the exhaust seeped in.

Years later, I joined Fred and his family for a road trip from Tulsa to Miami. They were to pick me up at Shreveport Airport at 10 a.m. Shreveport has two airports, so the trip moved into the next phase once we realized we were at different airports.

The minivan for the six of them was palatial. The baby was strapped in a Department of Transportation-approved child seat. We could move comfortably between the front, middle, and rear sections—no climbing over seats. Video machines abounded, and we joined in the baby's cassette music of It's a Small World. Over and over.

Not familiar with the extent of modern road trip logistics, after a few minutes, I asked him about the trip. Learning from the Mancation chapter, I knew the answers would be brief.

"Where are we going?"

"New Orleans first, then the Florida panhandle, then Orlando."

"Cool. Driving the whole way?"

"Yep."

"Where are we staying?"

Fred seemed nervous but kept his composure. There was a pause as he thought about my question, watching the road as he was driving. Something caught his eye.

"We're staying at a lodge."

"Cool. A lodge is good."

He kept driving. I saw a billboard for KOA, Campgrounds of America, a few minutes later. They were advertising campground lodges. It was different from what I thought of as a lodge, but some airlines and many hotels differ from what they make themselves out to be.

We pulled into the first KOA. Dick Creamer, the KOA grounds concierge, checked us in at the entrance gate. The cabins had two rooms, a front room with a table and a small kitchen counter. In the back room were bunk beds. They were decent, and on this trip, I was a passenger.

We did that for two nights. Bathrooms and showers were a five-minute walk past the snake and alligator swamps. We went for dinner at a catfish place since that seemed the thing to do. I ordered the alligator burger.

In Orlando, we stayed at the world's largest Motel Six. The thick orange shag carpet was an upgrade from the KOA concrete floor. I slept in the living room on the couch. My nephews slept on the pull-out sofa. The sink or toilet over-flowed, so the floor was soaked when I stepped barefoot from the couch onto the thick orange shag carpet. I felt like Steve Martin when he washed his face in the water of John Candy's underwear soaking in the bathroom sink.

My sister-in-law says this trip is where I introduced my brother to sunflower seeds while driving, now a mainstay of his driving excursions. It's hard to miss the thirty varieties of sunflower seeds at the highway rest stops.

Watching families travel is interesting. After 500 flights, I stopped having an issue with crying babies, kids kicking seats, and checked-out parents. Orlando flights are full of kids running seat-back tray table folding tests. Up and down. Up and down. Up and down. This is how things have become. So now, I fly through Tampa or West Palm Beach instead. Vegas will be filled with people going to have a party, drink, gamble, and let loose. It's okay.

Travelers to Europe and Asia seem more relaxed (long flight, calmer destination) than those going to Mexico and the Caribbean (short flight, sun, booze). I generally observe that behaviors among siblings and families traveling together differ depending on the destination. Drinking, shouting, and even a fistfight or two. All pre-Covid.

Fred and I returned to Anchorage after spending eight hours in Barrow. More time in Barrow would have been better. The Internet is slow owing to how far away the satellites fly over the equator. We drove north to Denali and south to Seward. We drive. Across Panama in a car. Cancun, Mexico. Las Vegas, Nevada. Melbourne to the 12 Apostles. Auckland to Rotorua. It's how we go.

QANTAS, Los Angeles-Sydney-Auckland-Melbourne-Sydney-Los Angeles

One of the most excellent perks of traveling for business is, at times, being able to bring someone along. Occasionally, credit card companies and airlines offer "two-for-one" fares that cost more than the usually cheapest but much less than two tickets.

As a consultant at the time, I needed to be in Sydney for just a few days, less time than I would spend flying. My work entailed helping clients find new ways to reduce costs, discover new products, and improve customer interactions. Customer Service is a universal opportunity waiting to be solved.

And so, I found myself a month away from going to Sydney with a free business-class ticket. A few phone calls later, and Fred was in. It turned out we'd be going during his birthday.

Australia is one of the leading travel destinations for Americans. Maybe it has to do with being a "cousin" country, both having histories leading from the United Kingdom, although Australia lasted longer. Or possibly the Outback having the "Wild West" feel or because of the Outback restaurant advertising. Or perhaps because Americans perceive Australia as "so far away" or "down under" and yet familiar. The Great Barrier Reef, Sydney, the largest Greek community outside of Greece in Melbourne, and New Zealand close enough are all excellent reasons to visit.

A few weeks later, we were on different flights heading to Sydney. Fred arrived first and checked into the hotel. My flight arrived twelve hours later due partly to a diversion to Brisbane because of early-morning fog at Sydney Airport, which I understand happens occasionally during the Spring.

I finally got to the hotel, showered, and went to the office. Fred checked out some local sites during the day, and we met up late for dinner. We ate meat pie and bought some Tam Tams on our way to the hotel. We were both exhausted.

I started the second day early, drank a lot of coffee to fight the jet lag, and worked late again. Fred had gone sightseeing, and we met again for dinner. Fish and Tam Tams. He told me all he had seen, where he walked, about the Sydney Bridge and asked if I wanted to climb to the top of it. Sure.

By the third day, Fred asked if I could come back early. He was tired of sight-seeing and wanted to talk. With my work driving my schedule, it was hard to say one way or the other. As it turned out, I finished earlier that day, and we met for a beer and dinner. After three days, Fred was resolved that I was only focused on my work and not spending time with him.

"It's hard to sightsee alone," he said.

Find a traveling buddy, and if you're fortunate to have a brother or sister who's a great traveling partner, you have it made.

His closing comment at dinner was, "Dude, I'm not your wife."

TAKE AWAY: How do we view others, and how do they view us? Developing lasting relationships creates safety, camaraderie, innovation, risk-taking, speed, and long-term stability.

PART III:
TRAVELING

I'M A TRAVELING MAN, I'VE BEEN EVERYWHERE, MAN.

I'm a Traveling Man, I've Been Everywhere, Man.
I've been to Dollywood, Wildwood, Sea World, and Disney World,
    but not to Wally World.
I've been to Hollywood; I've been to Redwood.
    I crossed the ocean for American Gold.
I've been to Bucharest, Budapest, and BuddaFest,
    but rarely do I get to take a rest.
When I can, I take a mancation, staycation, spacation,
    but never a vacation.
I've taken plenty of fakecations and occasionally take a workcation.

I've been to Manhattan, Manchuria, Manchester, and the Isle of Man,
    but not to Burning Man.
I've been Lost in Translation, Under the Tuscan Sun, Sideways,
    and spent a Midnight in Paris.
I've been Into the Wild and Out of Africa,
Up in the Air, Up in Smoke,
    and Down and Out in Beverly Hills.
As I look back and shed a tear,
    planes, trains, and automobiles were my career.

I've taken the Slow Boat to China and The Great Railway Bazaar;
I traveled with a Tangerine and Traveled with a Tsar.

Once, I nearly fell Off the Map, but I never fell off The Dancer's Lap
Took the Last Train to Istanbul but not the Last Train to Clarksville.

I Ate, Prayed, and Loved and Roughed It.
I Flew West with the Night, and I Danced in the Rain in New York.
I write with journal curled, marveling at What a Wonderful World.
I'm On the Road Again and Homeward Bound.

YOU ALWAYS REMEMBER YOUR FIRST (TRIP)

DC-9: Eastern Airlines, Miami–Fort Lauderdale
Cessna 150: Opa-locka
Hot-Air Balloon: Napa
Parachute: Bangkok
Bungee: Macau
Stunt plane flying upside down at 350mph: Las Vegas

My first trip was a few months after I was born.

The story was that my father, serving in the U.S. Coast Guard in the U.S., was due to return overseas for his next assignment. My mother was six months pregnant (with me) and not about to travel by ship, propeller planes, or both, which could take up to a week with good connections. My mother, father, brother, sister, and I traveled to Greece a few months after I was born.

I've met people born into an affluent lifestyle and those not during my travels. There are those born into families of exceptional talent, like talent is part of their DNA. I spoke with people who made a significant life out of poverty and those who ruined a life of great potential, although "ruined" seems too finite. Some find their gift regardless of how they are raised, and that gift becomes their life for the betterment of themselves and others.

We choose our life. Repeatedly, I read and hear of those who rise from a negative upbringing and those who fall from a positive upbringing. What makes the difference? Some give up early, as did one of my brothers. Another brother has schizophrenia. Chance and luck play a part. Somewhere along the way, we meet with the results of our choices.

After my father retired from the Coast Guard, my family moved back to Miami, along with my two additional younger brothers.

Ten years later, I met a plane.

Through a friend whose father owned a flying school, at 13, I took the first flight I remembered. It was in a Cessna named 9G. The smell of airplane fuel, the walking around the plane, the cramped space inside, the bouncing around while we taxied, communicating with the control tower, and the lineup and takeoff were not what a seventh grader could easily comprehend. But… I met a plane.

When I was 15, I took my first airline flight, 30 miles from Miami to Fort Lauderdale and back. I took the bus to the airport, walked to the ticket counter, bought my ticket, and walked to the gate with my ticket in the ticket jacket and a seat number written on the cover with a magic marker. No one asked if my parents knew. I experienced the smell of airplane seats and smoking on board, the window seat, taxiing, takeoff, landing, walking around the airport, and on the return. When I got home, my parents asked me what I had done. "Uh, nothing."

That night, I dreamt about meeting a plane.

Shortly after that, I started flying lessons at 15. I remember my logbook and the ground school sessions on weather and aerodynamics. I worked for Burger King to pay for my flight lessons, paying for each flight with cash. I flew around South Florida, practicing landings at different airports with the instructor.

I made my first flight alone at 16. The instructor put a rubber band around the microphone to ensure I could communicate if there were a problem. After I took off, I looked out the window and exclaimed, "I'm doing this. I'm flying alone!" The control tower guy asked if I was okay, so I undid the rubber band. I was flying by myself before I even had a driving license. I met a plane.

At an Irish pub my father frequented in Miami, he met a Pan Am captain leading a Fear of Flying course. The instructor, Captain (T.J.) Cunningham, invited me to join the class of twelve participants where each discussed their reason for being afraid to fly. In the course, Captain Cunningham explained the principles of flight, the different events that would happen, the noises, the computers involved, and the training required for each employee to perform their tasks.

In the 'live' part of the class, we walked around a parked Boeing 727. Flight attendants greeted us as we boarded the plane. We sat in the seats and buckled our seatbelts. At that point, one passenger left the plane, hyperventilating. The flight attendants served drinks and a snack as we sat motionless. In other classes, we visited the Pan Am offices, the training center, and the maintenance hangar and taxied around Miami International Airport in the Pan Am 727. Another passenger had to be let off the plane. The graduation flight was a trip from Miami around Key West and back. I empathized with the passengers, and the flight attendants captivated my attention. The smell inside the airplane is something I remember from time to time as I board a flight. I was sixteen.

My next flight would be to San Antonio for Air Force training and on to Japan, where I lived for three years. I flew on Air Force military cargo planes around the Pacific to Korea, the Philippines, Hawaii, Alaska, and Northern Japan. I rode Navy cargo planes up the Western U.S. coastline and back to Japan. Each trip was a new meeting, a new adventure.

In Macau, after I led a workshop on business risk, several of the staff reminded me that Macau is home to the world's tallest bungee from a building. I recalled seeing that on The Amazing Race. Why not? Off we went. It was raining, and somewhere around the 70th floor, the elevator broke through the clouds to the bungee platform. After I jumped—somewhere around the 10th floor on the way down, the cord started coming undone around my ankles. I'm here; that's a story for another book. It was another first in a couple of ways.

Learning is about looking for firsts. Outside of Las Vegas is a stunt flying school. Bruce was the pilot, and I told him I was a private pilot. Bruce let me try different configurations, like flying in a loop, flying upside down, flying up and down, and flying around the outside of a circle. These were the same planes used in the Red Bull air races worldwide. What an experience. I met a plane and a pilot without limit.

A few years later, I met Gabe, a hot-air balloon pilot who takes tourists around Napa Valley. Curious about his journey, I inquired how he entered this profession. He shared that he'd rise early during childhood to watch the balloons float over his house near Napa, chasing them as far as he could. During his teenage years, he transitioned into a 'chaser,' responsible for securing and carefully stowing the balloon and basket in a trailer after each landing. Eventually, he earned his hot air balloon pilot certificate, purchased a balloon, and launched his company. Every day, Gabe lives his dream.

Gabe told me his story while we were flying over a small town. Looking down, I saw a boy pointing up, squinting, and then running to follow us. The boy met a hot-air balloon.

In several parts of this book, I refer to looking out the airplane window and seeing a boy standing outside the airport fence, watching planes come and go, wondering who the people were on board. When I fly into Miami International Airport, I try to get a window seat on the right side when the planes land to the East. I look at the fence I used to stand at as the boy who wondered who the people were flying on these planes.

Dreams find us differently, and we can choose whether or not to follow them.

Travel seemed to find me.

I followed.

TAKE AWAY: I often reflect on past experiences that got me where I am. The book's title, What Got You Here Won't Get You There, sums up the next part of life's adventure. Still, as we check the rearview mirror from time to time, reflection is essential to show us how far we've come.

COOKIE

American Airlines, New York - Dallas

This is one of my favorite travel experiences with an unforeseen ending.

I can't say I've experienced love at first sight, but there have been moments when I came close. I've felt infatuation a few times. I've heard of people who actively seek the anticipation of being in love, and for some, friendships and relationships develop unexpectedly. Much remains unspoken and assumed, but that's part of the magic.

I was between marriages and not paying attention to my relational life. That was the key: not paying attention. Years later, I am still humored by what caught me so off guard. This may be what happens. We don't get to pick what or when something or someone affects us.

Her name was Cookie.

I traveled 200 days a year, worked ten-hour days, and didn't feel a strong need for another person to be close to in my life. My life was a whirlwind of scattered pieces just on the brink of being out of control—like Dorothy when she was in the tornado. Fence posts and boxes flying by. Then, a chicken and a goat. A cow. A house. The witch riding her bicycle, "I'll get you and your dog."

Just like that, I gave myself to my work. I traveled as often as possible. I visited as many clients as I could. I had a desk at the home office but rarely saw it. It sometimes overwhelmed me, but the people I worked with cared for me. They lightened the load, and I felt safe.

On this trip, I traveled to New York to present my part of a multimillion-dollar sales pitch to a large client. These presentations could be exhausting. Not only did we have to understand what the customer needed, but we had to show how our products could improve their and clients' lives.

Salespeople always hang out on a branch, looking to close the next deal. Customers wonder if the product is really what is being sold. Employees want to know that the product will work; bosses want to know that the product is profitable. I just wanted to know that the customer, the employee team, the product, and the business aligned.

I learned that my boss and company had promoted me before my presentation. I was now a vice president at a Fortune 500 company. More pay. More clients. And more travel. More time on the road. More exhaustion. More nights in hotels that seemed to blur together. More fast breakfasts. More boxed lunches. More dinners. No slowing down.

Sensing this, my colleagues invited me to dinner at a nice restaurant that evening. They genuinely cared about me.

I returned to my hotel, showered, and changed. Business dinners were usually right after work, nothing fancy. The main guy was a New Yorker and told me where to go and when to be there. I hailed a cab and cabbie who dropped me off in an unfamiliar area. I was looking forward to dinner and relaxing.

I checked in at the greeting stand. I was late, but the attractive maitre d' was friendly and told me not to worry. I felt embarrassed at being the last one in my party to arrive. She walked me to our table. The rest of the group were already drinking and laughing. I lightened up. I felt like I could exhale. It was a U-shaped table, and my six colleagues sat in pairs on each side. I took the only remaining chair, a lone seat in the aisle.

And then Cookie arrived.

Like hitting a brick wall, time slowed, then stopped. Cookie gently pulled my knees slightly apart and sat on my leg. What was happening?

The rest of the table was good with it like this was normal. I looked around. No one else seemed to think anything was amiss. This restaurant was nice but must have had an overly friendly wait staff as a twist. Perhaps my group told Cookie this was a congratulations dinner, and I had a tough day.

Cookie was funny. She spoke slowly, asking each person about their next drink order. She had a great voice and probably recited menu specials with suggestions on what was exceptional. She was deliberate. She put her arm around me, pulled me close, and whispered her name. I froze. She took my drink order. It was all too quick, and as quick as she was there, she was gone.

My colleagues carried on as usual. They all worked for the head of customer sales, the guy to my right. Next to him was the account manager. On the back wall were a couple of techie guys. And to the left of me were two more account support guys. We discussed the day, the customer, and what was next. We felt the meeting went well and breathed with relief.

A short time later, Cookie returned, put my drink on the table, and pulled my knees apart so she could sit down again. She was a lightweight and seemed to float. As she slowly took everyone else's dinner order, she offered to order for me. We talked for a moment. She whispered. I looked into her eyes, and she left to put in our order.

I was struck for sure, and I wasn't sure how.

More chitchat at our table. It didn't seem to matter. Cookie returned to tell us about ourselves, starting with the main guy.

"You're the boss."

"Yes."

Next. "You're a hardened New Yorker."

"Yes."

Next. "You're closeted."

"Close, but not closeted."

Next. "You're in a committed relationship."

"Yes."

Next. "You two are in a relationship together."

"Indeed."

Her voice quickened with each disclosure. She was mysterious and attractive, and her mannerisms were lively. Maybe it was her wit, friendly acceptance of others, her dreams, or her joy of doing a job that she loved. She was young but street-smart. She crossed her legs as she sat on my lap. I felt somehow that Cookie knew how to make people feel special. She told us that Cookie was a working name since customers could get overly friendly, and it was a way to protect herself.

We ate our dinner, and Cookie checked on us occasionally, resting her hand softly on my shoulder. Her white t-shirt hugged her top. Her jeans showed the rest of her figure. Her hands were soft like her voice.

After dinner, Cookie returned to chat with the others at our table. She was good. She studied people intently. From our conversation, I learned that people have ranges of habits, ranges of likes and dislikes, ranges of fun and work, and even thoughts of themselves. It was like a dinner in social psychology. That conversation ended with all of us fitting in somewhere.

During dessert, Cookie came back for a final visit. She tapped my knee and sat lightly on my leg. I told her I had a 6 a.m. flight back home. She slipped her phone number into my shirt pocket and asked me to call the next time I was in town if I wanted to. As she left, she whispered in my ear once again.

When I returned to my office on Monday morning, there was an 18-inch chocolate chip cookie with bright yellow writing for my coworkers to see, "Love, Cookie." It was a surprising reminder of my dinner a few evenings before.

I looked at the cookie and contemplated breaking off a piece. I remembered her sitting on my lap. Her laugh. Her voice. Her charm. Her conversation.

And I thought of what Cookie whispered as she left our table.

"Jim, I'm a man."

TAKE AWAY: Laugh at your life adventures (or misadventures). Reflect on them with positivity. Only some things will turn out how you want or expect, which is OK. Respect others whose shoes we have not walked in. Appreciate your colleagues. Ask them why things seem to be going wrong for them or not in their direction. Make it part of the discussion so there can be learning and acceptance. That is an epiphany waiting to happen!

9/11

JetBlue, Long Beach-Boston
American Airlines, London-Dallas

My roll-aboard suitcase sat naked in the security area, emptied and taken apart. It was 9/11, and for a few years after 2001, I'd made it a point to fly on this day to celebrate my freedom. Even with the extra security, bag and body searches, other passengers' trepidation, and questioning from friends and family.

I have a packing system. I pack clean socks and shorts inside my shoes on my outbound flights to keep my shoes from crushing. I neatly fold my dirty clothes and slide them into a plastic hotel laundry bag on my return flights. Whatever I can shove into my shoes to keep them from crushing is what I put in them. I screwed up this trip by packing an electric razor, a trimmer, and a battery charger into my shoes for my return flight from England to the U.S.

It embarrassed me when the security lady unpacked my bag, touching each item and feeling for something out of place. She lifted out the shirt I would wear upon returning to the U.S., my ties, dress shirts, and pants. She took out the plastic laundry bag and looked inside my homemade hamper. I told her they were dirty clothes. She said something about her husband and went about her job.

I was sweating.

A husband, wife, and 10-year-old daughter of the family that was in the line behind me were looking at my stuff.

The security lady, Linda (by now, we were on a first-name basis), took out some magazines, my hairbrush, comb, clean underclothes (since I always bring exactly one extra day's worth of clean under-clothes), deodorant (since it doesn't have to go in the three ounce-only liquids bag), and a pair of worn jeans. I was glad I packed my liquids in my backpack.

An aged couple in dual wheelchairs was next, looking at me like I did something wrong or was going to do something wrong. They were hoping I was not on their flight.

Linda got into the bag with my dress shoes. She slid them out of the black Virgin Atlantic shoe bag and asked if I had anything in my shoes.

"Yes."

She took out the plastic bag with my battery-powered razor, hair trimmer, and the battery charger for my digital camera. My suitcase was empty, but not enough for Linda.

A business person passed by, relieved that the "security lady" was all over my bag and not his. That's how I think.

Linda's hand slid through the Velcro-attached suitcase liner and took it apart, looking for something else. I told her there was a zipper compartment on the side where I keep band-aids, duct tape, an extra cell phone connector, a spare comb, Advil, Imodium, and some cold medicine. She was looking for the connector.

A lady with a Chanel roll-aboard and matching handbag was next. Her roll-aboard was over-packed, overweight, and would not have lasted as a checked bag underneath the plane.

Linda returned my bag to the security line's beginning for another pass-through. Satisfied there was nothing else to pick through, she left it and left me.

And there it sat at the end of the conveyor belt. I must have been stunned because when Linda returned, she looked at me like everything I owned sat in a pile on a cold metal table, like a lifeless body on Dateline. The husband did it.

Another family passed by with an infant, a four-year-old, and a baby seat for the flight. They had a lot of stuff. I moved my pile so they could collect their things, careful not to pack their baby formula.

I rolled the magazines back into my bag. I left the electronics out since I knew I would again go through security for my connecting flight. I refolded my clothes.

I love my freedom. Four of my brothers and I were in the U.S. Air Force—worldwide. They served in Germany, Turkey, the Netherlands, Alaska, Nevada, and Texas; I was in Japan and California. My nephews are in the U.S. Coast Guard and U.S. Air Force. My father was in the U.S. Coast Guard, as was one of his brothers and my cousin.

While in the U.S. Air Force in Japan, I visited Iwo Jima. That's where the Marine Corps War Memorial in Washington, D.C., shows a group of U.S. Marines raising the American flag during World War II. I flew with Charlie, a C-130 navigator. When I visited Iwo-Jima, it was a U.S. Coast Guard LORAN station providing navigational guidance around the Pacific Ocean. The weekly C-130 delivered mail, food, and supplies. I was the only non-worker on the plane.

I visited Mount Suribachi, the place depicting the raising of the flag, one of the highest casualty engagements for the US Marines during World War II. The sulfuric gas oozing from a nearby pit was like sticking my head in a bag of old eggs. I collected a glass ball that washed ashore and was used to weigh down fishing nets. Around that time, they had just uncovered the bones of a deceased soldier from World War II on the island. A few hours later, we packed the return mail and returned to the Japanese main island and our base.

Years later, my son and I flew from the Philippines to Guam to visit my Coast Guard nephew and his wife. My son and I dived into a harbor to explore the reef. The water was perfect, and the sea life was incredible.

The next day, we flew to Hawaii via Chuuk, Pohnpei, Kwajalein, and Majuro. The Boeing 737 carried spare parts and extra crew members because of the flight length, owing to each stop. Each place reminded me of the possibility that my father visited during World War II.

Thank you, Linda, and the people whose daily job is to ensure we're safe. As I stared at the rest of my stuff on the metal table, I felt safer since Linda was thorough.

Then she looked at me sadly.

I went to the plane behind an old guy being pushed in a wheelchair. He wasn't in a hurry.

Neither was I.

I travel.

I made it a point to travel on 9/11 in memory of those who can't.

TAKE AWAY: The terrorist attacks in the US on September 11, 2001, changed the lives of Americans and many others worldwide. Increased safety and security became the norm. The key is to remember, to give thanks, and to offer compassion to those doing their jobs to protect us.

NIGHT TRAINS

Los Angeles - Seattle
Beijing - Lhasa
Istanbul - Sofia
Sofia - Bucharest
Bucharest - Belgrade
Belgrade - Budapest
Paris - Zurich
Seattle - Chicago
Chicago - Emeryville
Genoa - Naples
Narvik – Stockholm

9:00 a.m., Bucharest.

I was drinking coffee at the café and writing notes about my train trip with my brother, Fred. This was day four of an eight-day Eastern Europe trip on overnight trains. We figured we could eat, sleep, and move simultaneously to save money.

Outside, the temperature was nearly freezing, and it was raining. It was slushy. I was wet, cold, and hungry and decided to spend the first part of the day at a day hotel after two nights on the train.

After coffee, we caught a train to the airport so Fred could fly to Amsterdam for his mother-in-law's funeral. He was close with his wife's family, and I could tell it weighed heavily on him. We hugged as he left the airport train station for the airline check-in desk. I watched a pack of wild dogs walking along the tracks while I waited for a train back to the city center.

A few months earlier, I told Fred that I wanted to take the trains from Istanbul to Vienna along the route of the Orient Express; he said he was game. We talked about what we would do in Istanbul for three days and how it was somewhere we both had an interest in visiting. We shared research. A Turkish friend told me that the locals loved to bargain—the more two people argued, the greater the respect. To me, it sounded like there were going to be significant arguments.

All my brothers were born on Rhodes, the closest Greek island to Turkey. The Ottomans (Turks) occupied Rhodes from 1523-1912, and the Turkish and Middle Eastern influence still influences architecture and spas. My next younger brother's godfather owned a hotel in Rhodes City where you can see Turkey from the balcony. We grew up drinking Turkish coffee and eating lamb and plenty of baklava.

My mother's immigration to the U.S. and my ethnic upbringing reminded me that we are just one generation removed from elsewhere.

Fred and I met up in London for our flight to Istanbul. He booked the hotel and the three or four places we would visit. Upon arrival at the Istanbul Atatürk Airport, we got in line to buy our visa ($20), then in line for passport control, then in line for customs before being hit by a wall of cigarette smoke and a gaggle of taxi drivers, each wanting to drive us to town.

Fred, shrewd by DNA and aware of the bargaining rule, went from driver to driver, yelling (negotiating) and walking away. I thought we were going to have to walk. He decided to make the drivers sweat, so we sat for a cup of thick Turkish coffee. The Camel cigarette smoke looked impenetrable. Afterward, Fred got the taxi price down from 70 Euros ($100+) to 18 Euros ($25), but we would ride in a van with another couple and make their stop before ours. Give a little, take a lot—that was his motto.

Some countries should ban drivers.

It was late and raining when we finally arrived at our hotel in the historic part of town. We had traveled nearly 24 hours, and Fred was tired of airplane and airport food. We threw down our luggage and walked to the train station to get our train tickets. The train station ticket window for our onward journey was closed.

We walked a few blocks in the rain, checking the restaurant prices. At each restaurant, the maître d' told us how good their food is; at the next restaurant, they told us how good their food is. We decided on a place where Fred negotiated two free beers and complimentary tea. It's unbelievable what deals one can make.

Back at the hotel, we tried to sleep—the 5 a.m. Adhan Muslim Call to Prayer played over the loudspeakers, calling the Muslim faithful to pray. After, we walked to the train station, went to the information window, and said we needed reservations to Sofia. We were told we had to go to the ticket window, which would not be open until after lunch.

Across the street from the train station is the ferry to the Asian side of Istanbul. The Bosporus River is where Asia and Europe officially meet. We checked out a few of the ferries, wondering where they went. Choosing one, we went across the Bosporus to Asia, walked around, took in the sights, had a more Middle Eastern lunch that Fred negotiated with extra falafel and cacik (Turkish tzatziki), and took the ferry back.

The train ticket window person was at lunch when we got back. While waiting, we took in the Hagia Sophia, the Christian church built during Constantine's reign, afterward converted to a mosque, the Blue Mosque. We got lost in the Grand Bazaar, which has over 4,000 permanent shop sellers all under multiple roofs cobbled together and does not include the 1,000 more shops outside the Bazaar. We rode the tram and took a cab (Fred negotiated 50% off the cab rate) back to the hotel.

At dinner, we watched the Dervish dancers twirl endlessly. We ate more lamb and cacik and drank Efes beer that Fred could get thrown in. It was entertaining, as were the Dervish twirlers.

We made each event an experience.

We returned to the train station the following day to buy our tickets for the train that night. They cost €68 each plus €27 for the sleepers, less than a hotel room. Bingo. Fred was proud.

The Bosporus Express.

Istanbul's Sirkeci Station was at one end of the Orient Express rail line, with the other end being Paris or London. The Sirkeci café and Orient Express sign were still there. The waiting room looked as it had for a century: old seats, worn tile floors, and stucco walls. Although the station is now closed for train travel, visiting it would still be well worth it.

Mike and Susan, honeymooners from Vancouver traveling with her mother, told us we'd have to pay to leave Turkey. They weren't sure since they were Canadian and we were American. As we learned, this was one time it didn't cost extra to be American or travel with mom.

After our last Turkish coffee at the station cafe, we boarded the 22:00 Bosporus Express for Sofia. After the engine and mail car, the passenger cars were two worn-out Bulgarian and Romanian rail cars heading to Bucharest and two new Turkish sleeper cars heading to Sofia. While taking the train, it is essential to be in the right rail car at the right time; otherwise, when the train cars separate and go to different destinations, you could be in for a different adventure.

Our cabin had bunk beds, with Fred taking the high road since he was younger. We were wet and cold, so we both sat on the cabin heater while it was warming up.

Thick tobacco smoke filled the train car passage. We opened the outside window as we got in our beds to sleep. I felt we were in the Agatha Christie book, Murder on the Orient Express. *"All around us are people, of all classes, of all nationalities, of all ages. For three days, these people, these strangers to one another, are brought together. They sleep and eat under one roof; they cannot get away from each other. At the end of three days they part, they go their several ways, never, perhaps, to see each other again."*

The Bosporus Express left on time. For the first five hours, we tried to sleep to the feel of the train wheels riding over the equivalent of rail-line potholes and clicking between the rail-line gaps.

The cabin heater worked too well or not at all. The window stayed open or closed when we hit a wide rail gap.

Seven hours after we left Istanbul, someone banged on the door so we could attend the border crossing process. We got dressed, walked in the snow on the platform, down through a dark, damp tunnel under the tracks, and up the stairs to the immigration building, where we waited in line for 20 minutes with the other sleepy passengers. The Turkish Border Patrol agent looked at my passport and then on to the next window for me. I filled out the eight-page questionnaire on everything I did and spent in Turkey; Fred didn't.

Back outside, down the stairs, through the tunnel, which now had a big barking dog, up the stairs, through the snow to our cabin. We changed back into sleeping clothes and went back to sleep.

Twenty minutes later, the Turkish customs officer came through, checking for artifacts being taken out of the country. A gander through our luggage and all was well.

Back to sleep, train rolling. Twenty minutes later, all stopped, and the Bulgarian conductor showed up, asking for tickets, which I had given to the Turkish conductor. All good.

The wake-up drill started seeming comical, so after changing clothes three times, we returned to our beds in shorts. This was a regular thing, taking the train between countries not grouped in the same economic zone. Back to sleep.

Right on time, twenty minutes later, the Bulgarian immigration officer showed up to collect our passports. I handed them over. Twenty minutes later, I heard a lady outside and decided it would be wise to put my pants back on. Good thing. "You nice A-merr-i-KAN boys."

What should have been a 10:50 a.m. arrival to Sofia turned into an arrival later in the afternoon. Another tip—try not to book back-to-back train trips with tight connections. While it might be fun to miss a train – it's another story to get back on schedule, find a cabin available, and reschedule all the connections.

The station was sad. The snow was blowing, no heat or lights, and it was dark. Dark concrete. Dark stairs. Dark, broken tile. Large and nondescript. Sofia, it turned out, is a gorgeous city.

The first thing we had to do was to ensure we had reservations for our train that evening. Off to the first ticket window. Then, to the international ticket window. Then, to the Eurail ticket window.

Since my rail pass didn't allow me to travel to Bulgaria, I had to pay for a ticket. Fred's was okay—total price: €90. No negotiating. The good thing was that the three-person cabin was half the price, and the lady said they rarely put three people in a cabin. Tickets in hand, we ventured outside the station.

The snow turned into a blizzard. Snow was piling up, the wind was howling, and daytime darkness began enveloping us. We walked through the massive once-grand Soviet-era dark concrete train station entrance and found a cafe serving food. Fred got the meat in lentil soup, and I opted for the frozen chicken leg and equally frozen mashed potatoes—total price: 13 Liv ($8).

At lunch, a man heard us talking about going into town and offered to help. His train station friend offered to take us to a taxi, explain where we wanted to go and help us get on the metro line. Once we got in the taxi, he blocked the door until we tipped him 5 Liv ($3). The taxi, equally a rip-off, took us to the closest metro station, 13 Liv ($8) a block away.

We bought two metro tickets, 5 LIV ($1.50 each) for the one-stop ride into town. We checked out the Saint Sofia Church (city center) and some high-end shops (Gucci, etc.) to avoid freezing.

The city center was magical. Stringed holiday lights, probably year-round, kept the streets lit up. The townsfolk dressed well, bundled up in the falling snow. Between the snow, water, and lights, it was as though someone had placed a camera filter that made the lights twinkle even more. Fred and I jumped into another café.

We traveled during the less-traveled time of the year, which is typical for us. It's an excellent way to avoid crowds, pay less money for hotels and food, and make our own pace. Of course, you have less optimal weather, fewer open restaurants, and more closed stores.

A cup of coffee and some jam-filled cookies later, and we returned to the train station for our trip to Romania. The tram should have cost 5 Liv ($3) for the two of us, but since the ticket window was closed and we boarded, we had to pay a 13 Liv ($8) penalty each. Ouch. We argued with the tram cop, but that didn't work. A few other riders told the tram cop to let us go, but that didn't work, either.

At the station, we waited downstairs, where the wind blew the least. We shivered with the other fifty or so people going to destinations north and east. West was Kosovo, Macedonia, and Albania; south were Greece and Turkey, with trains on the other track.

Many people carried plastic, shopping, paper, or roll-aboard bags. Some had food. Most of them smoked Bulgarian cigarettes in the dark, confining space. The smoke clung to our clothes. There were young and old, and everyone made it work. It was good to see people traveling; however, they decided to go. Without a doubt, train people travel very differently than those on planes.

The Bulgaria Express

The Bulgaria Express traveled daily between Sofia and Moscow via Bucharest. A couple hundred soldiers boarded the rail cars going toward Moscow. The rest of the rail cars were going elsewhere. Being in the right rail car on this trip was super important.

We got to our car. I checked the signage and found the right door. A not-to-be-messed-with Bulgarian conductor guarded the doorway. While friendly, I felt like we were already in trouble. Any number of things could be wrong. She checked our tickets and let us board.

We quickly found our cabin. Mahogany wood lined the walls. We had a shower at one end, a porcelain sink, and bunk beds. They spectacularly made the beds with nicely pressed sheets. The conductor lady came by to collect our tickets, and the train left Sofia right on time at 7:30 p.m.

Even though it was early when we left, we fell right asleep, knowing that we would arrive in Bucharest at 5:44 a.m. The beds had new cushions, the cabin was warm and comfortable, and the tracks were quiet.

At about 1:00 a.m., the same conductor and two other conductors, a boy and a woman, woke us with ticket problems. My first ticket was for the domestic portion since my Bulgaria segment was not included initially. And my rail pass included Romania.

Fred's pass included Bulgaria, and when I showed that to the three conductors, the conductor in charge whacked the boy and told him in Russlish that he was "stoopit" and to get out of her sight. She mumbled an apology and slammed our door closed. I heard the door lock from the outside.

Two hours later, the Bulgarian passport crew showed up to stamp our passports, followed in twenty-minute increments by customs, Romanian immigration, and Romanian customs visits. We arrived in Bucharest at 8:00 a.m., just over two hours late, in time for a cup of $1 coffee, airport tickets for Fred and me, and a train ticket for me to go to Belgrade that evening.

After deciding that two days on the train, snow, no snow clothes, getting ripped off, and having some alone time, I got a day room at the hotel two blocks away. Taxi drivers offered to take me, but I was ready to walk. I checked in, showered, ate breakfast, and drank coffee.

While not much in the way of travel surprises me, I arrived in time to watch a "Dating-by-Correspondence" convention. It seemed a combination of speed dating, interrogation, and musical chairs. Everyone seemed to have a good time.

That night, I began my solo trip to the capital of Serbia, Belgrade—first, a change of trains at Timisoara in the middle of the night. No sleeper.

The station platform for the train to Timisoara was filled with young people, probably because there are multiple universities there. Most of them seemed to be models, wholly impeccable. Not one type of clothing, hair color, or style, just a sea of perfection. What caught my attention was that they were all speaking English.

When I travel, I carry a few months of unread newspapers to catch up on. One was sticking out of my bag, and three students asked me if I was English. We talked about the university, Timisoara being like a frontier city, their dream to travel and live abroad, and if I needed help. I was happy that they wanted to go.

A good sleep and time to change trains – twice, plus another border crossing. Some borders are about getting off the train (Turkey - Bulgaria and France - Switzerland). Some trains do the process while moving between countries. And sometimes, there is one platform with the train from each country on either side. That's how this one went between Romania and Serbia. There was no building, the connecting train had not arrived, and it was getting colder.

After about 30 minutes, a local train showed up. I should have taken it as a sign that there were going to be a lot of stops. The 1½ hour train to connect to Budapest took nearly 4 hours because of railway construction—an amateur mistake on my part. I could have switched trains a few stations earlier.

All was not lost. The Belgrade Station was one stop on the Orient Express train line. I asked the ticket agent to rebook my connection and then about the original train. She pointed me to a small area serving as an Orient Express Museum. Model trains, uniforms, photos of famous people, maps. Bonus!

Between Europe and the Middle East, Serbia and Serbian food was memorable. The food was similar to Greek (meat from smaller animals), but I noticed more continental types of meat, including pork, beef, and venison. They served dinner as a pie, as was the dessert. A cup of coffee later, I returned to the station to go to Budapest and connect with Fred.

Trains are magical. Because people are in proximity for more extended periods, or as a slower pace of transportation, or something more earthy, the traveler comes away with a very different experience when they disconnect from faster ways of traveling.

Night trains add another layer of "difference," as do longer-distance trains. You miss the scenery of daytime travel, more opportunities to meet others and converse, and possibly some meals. Also, sleeping while moving might be hard for some. The tracks are not welded on older rail lines so that the noise could be bothersome.

One would only find each of these while taking the night train.

TAKE AWAY: Do different things. Do things differently. Immerse yourself in the experience. I marvel at movies that draw us in such that we live the story without leaving our chairs. Travel is similar, except we are IN the experience. We should be present in our personal and business lives. And we should move ahead with confidence.

ROAD WARRIOR, ROAD WEARIER

American Airlines, Chicago–Santa Ana

> *"Why anyone should desire to visit either Luc or Cheylard is more than my much-inventing spirit can suppose. **For my part, I travel not to go anywhere, but to go. I travel for travel's sake. The great affair is to move;** to feel the needs and hitches of our life more nearly; to come down off this feather-bed of civilisation, and find the globe granite underfoot and strewn with cutting flints. Alas, as we get up in life, and are more preoccupied with our affairs, even a holiday is a thing that must be worked for. "*
>
> – Robert Louis Stevenson, *Travels with a Donkey in the Cevennes*

The day I traveled one million miles, I thought it was a milestone that would happen only once in my life. I have learned to find the best flights and hotels, take side trips to unknown places, meet great people, and sleep upright before takeoff.

250,000 Miles

A Road Warrior sounds like a traveler battling with everything in their way— the hazards of frequent travel and its demands. In the early 2000s, American Airlines' American Way magazine held an annual contest for their most frequent travelers, the road warriors. There's no doubt that frequent travel eventually takes a toll on us.

Road Warriors can find cheaper flights and hotel rooms, find the shortest lines at customs, and pack three weeks of clothing in a roll-aboard suitcase or backpack. These are more like Travel Ninjas. We watch and learn from each other about new tips and tricks on traveling in what way works for us.

The internet is replete with sources, tips, tricks, what to say and not say to a flight attendant, what the flight attendant is looking for when you board, what is wrong with ice cubes and coffee on planes, why the lavatory is not the dirtiest place on a plane, how to join the mile-high club, how to score an upgrade (not that easy), which booking site will save you a dollar or two, credit card points, top-10 things to see anywhere, last-minute cruises, why women should not wear leggings or shorts on a plane and videos of winning emergency briefings (Air New Zealand for their highly regarded Hobbit and naked crew member briefings).

And yet, with all of that, travel is still a mystery to most, including the Road Warrior.

Road Warriors come in all sizes and shapes. We congregate around the boarding areas, eyeing one another. We avoid the "travel ignorant who don't know the rules" (another Up in the Air reference). These "rules" change with each airline, hotel, car company, cruise, rideshare, and, as we experienced with COVID-19, with each country. We claw to access the precious overhead space to store our baggage so we don't have to wait for what seems like hours for our bag at the baggage carousel. I've probably saved half a life by not checking baggage during that part of my life when carry-on was the "rule."

We check our frequent-travel accounts more religiously than we check our bank accounts. Each of the multiple airlines, hotel chains, car rental companies, and credit card point accounts to navigate maximizing the point conversion between them. It's exhausting and thrilling at the same time.

500,000 Miles

I saw a skinny kid the other day looking up at the sky, wondering where a particular plane was going, who was on it, and how they got there so that one day, he could too. I hoped he would realize his dream and be on that plane as some other little boy or girl looked up at him.

For many Road Warriors, "the journey is the destination" is a cliche. More miles, hotel nights, and car rentals become an addiction. Frequent traveler websites with hundreds of thousands of members are each primed to share their experience so someone else can follow. On one website, travel diehards upload pictures of airline food from the few airlines that serve food.

The TSA checker knows my name. A flight attendant gave me her phone number since we live near each other, so we could drive together to the airport since we both flew the same overnight flight each week. The airline club agent, who knew I only had 75 minutes between flights, held a shower for me in Miami. Road Warriors know the villagers.

750,000 Miles

Traveling is dirty. News shows discuss what's left behind on the hotel blanket, how the room attendants don't wash the in-room glasses very well, people who clean their underclothes in the hotel hot pot, or the germs on airplane bathroom faucets, tray tables, and seat back pockets—or getting into a dirty, smelly cab (but, not in London).

Road Warriors wait for the next plane, spend sleepless days and nights while our bodies argue with us over what time zone we should be in, change the time on our analog watch, flipflop on keeping the cell phone on local or at-home time, Outlook calendar time zones, lousy food, diarrhea, packing and unpacking, wrinkled clothes, no irons or automobile air-conditioning, tiny hotel rooms in France, foul smokers in Greece (I'm Greek), driving alone, sleeping alone, drinking alone, eating alone, all while around other people.

It's always just about the next mile.

One Million Miles

I arrived at the airport just like I did any other day I traveled, an hour before my flight. I parked my car in the same general area. In the days before cell phone boarding passes, you spoke with someone, showed them your identification, they typed into a computer, and a boarding pass came out of a printer.

On this day, as usual, the ticket counter agent asked me where I was going. Since I was traveling to two or three destinations each week for months, I drew a blank. I said, "I don't know where I'm going. I know I'm supposed to be on a flight at 7:30 a.m. A phone call later (maybe to my therapist), the agent found my reservation, and I was on my way to St. Louis. Nowadays, it's just on our mobile phones.

There are various tolls that frequent travelers pay for being on the journey. Just one generation ago, traveling abroad could take weeks of traveling on ships and trains. My grandparents took even longer—or they didn't travel.

Pilot Captain Mark Vanhoenacker invented the term "place lag" in his book Skyfaring: A Journey with a Pilot. Place lag is *the imaginative drag that results from our jet age displacements over every kind of distance; from the inability of our deep old sense of place to keep up with our aeroplanes.*" We need to reconnect where and when.

In an interview with The Guardian, Vanhoenacker describes it this way, *"Place lag is as unavoidable as jet lag, but it's far more interesting. Even wondrous, occasionally."*

The traveler of the past had to make time for travel, often arriving a day or two early to wait for the train or the ship, leaving enough time for error or delays. They stayed at local hotels, visited places along the way, ate the local food, and spoke to the people. It forced them to make time. It forced them to stop.

As I write, I think of how often my "rest" meant spending 20 minutes eating alone at a Taco Bell, McDonald's, or AuBonPain or drinking coffee at an airport coffee shop. Or dashing through the airport for a flight about to leave, jumping over chairs with my garment bag (wait, that was someone else). Or walking away from the gate, dejected from missing a flight two minutes too late, only to perk up when realizing the adventure is back on. Or getting the last seat on an earlier flight—in front of the exit row in the middle seat that doesn't recline.

I boarded my flight to St. Louis, happy to go somewhere again, but I realized I was getting tired. I have met many weary travelers, exhausted from hassling with the airline, with their luggage, with security, with the gate agent, with other passengers trying to get on the plane and to their seats, weary of the flight attendant, a long flight, or a screaming baby.

Traveling is a lot of work. After having been home for a year, I realize that more, driving to places with great names, like Dublin, Paris, Naples, and Moscow, all in Texas. Kingston, in Oklahoma. And Johannesburg, in California.

Waking up in a different city every few days, unpacking and re-packaging, is not a terrific way to experience the world. I spent a large part of my life trying to remember which hotel I was staying at or which room I was in or embarrassing myself by asking the receptionist. Add to that which rental car I was driving, and the weariness list keeps growing.

The worst times, though, were being startled awake in the morning by my cell phone alarm and staring wide-eyed at the ceiling with a rush of adrenaline.

"Where am I?"

"What day is this?"

"Why am I here?"

I was tired, panicked, and anxious, and I felt lost and helpless while staring at the ceiling that I had closed my eyes to the night before and not remembering where—place lag.

I was home.

TAKE AWAY: Whether it is travel or something else unrelated, we tire. Indicators may show themselves. The key is to pay attention, not quit, and not give up on ourselves, our colleagues, or our families.

PILGRIM

Iberia Airlines, Santiago de Compostela – Madrid

> *"In each of us dwells a wanderer, a gypsy, a pilgrim. The purpose here is to call forth that spirit. What matters most on your journey is how deeply you see, how attentively you hear, and how richly the encounters are felt in your heart and soul. Kabir wrote, 'If you have not experienced something, then for you it is not real. So it is with pilgrimage.'"*
>
> – Phil Cousineau. Art of Pilgrimage: The Seeker's Guide to Making Travel Sacred

I was returning home after walking across Spain on the Camino de Santiago. My feet had boils and blisters the size of half-dollars. I lost nearly 20 pounds, and I was tired. I walked alone. I hurt from pain and exhaustion almost the entire way back.

Since reading The Alchemist a few years earlier, I was increasingly driven to search for my life's purpose. In the book, Paulo Coelho, the author, wrote about finding one's personal legend and destiny, and I had just finished rereading this part. Coelho's first book, The Pilgrimage, is his memoir of his El Camino walk, so I decided this was an experience I needed. I needed something that would force me to stop and look within. It was during my walk that my life intention changed.

After watching a video of a couple who walked the Camino with their baby in a stroller and after reading Shirley McLain's book, The Camino, I felt confident I, too, could make it.

My wife bought me a backpack, a pair of boots, and a plane ticket to Spain. I loaded the pack with books and put on the boots. I hiked around our suburban neighborhood for eight hours on Saturdays and Sundays, breaking in my boots and adjusting to the backpack weight. Bikers waved, police officers followed, and colleagues doubted. I was on a mission. A few people offered money or food, thinking I was unhomed.

My family questioned my seriousness, having spoken of walking the Camino for a few years. I responded that I would rather have more things to do and not get to all of them than have a few things to do and cover them all.

I bought a travel book with suggested routes and places to stay. I would not be starting from the beginning since I did not have the full 30 days off from my work, which is the average time it takes. I studied the map, worked backward, and figured out where to start.

Just after my birthday, I left for Madrid, Spain. I boarded a train at the airport, changed at the central station downtown, then went north to Astorga on the path to Santiago. I found a small hotel near the edge of the town. The room was old, small, and uncomfortable—probably ideal for people walking.

On the small bed, I emptied my backpack. On the bed now was my flip phone, a quick-dry set of clothes, a pair of Teva sandals, a quick-dry towel, a sleeping bag liner, my CD player, twenty-four CDs of Wally Lamb's book, This Much I Know Is True, my El Camino guidebook, a little journal, and 48 food bars.

I was restless. After a short sleep, I woke just before sunrise, confident about where I was going.

I wandered around the city for the next two hours, lost. Stores were not open yet. A dog that only understood Spanish nearly bit me. I found a gas station, asked for directions, and got on my way.

Quickly, I learned to follow the yellow arrows. I put on my headphones, turned on the CD player, and listened to Wally Lamb.

I met a man from Madrid who walked the Camino every few years. His English was better than my Spanish. He carried a rucksack with sandwiches, toiletries, and underclothes. He told me he walked because he is Catholic, and it is part of his faith.

After 30 minutes, he peeled away, and I walked alone again, naturally.

I refilled my water bottle. I grabbed a sandwich at a supermarket and ate alone. I stayed in a hostel that night and took a cold shower since most hostels seemed not to have hot water. That first night, I cursed silently at already having blisters. I was on my way.

The next day, I visited a pharmacy. My blisters were bleeding. Someone had recently invented molecular-level bandages that stayed attached until the skin cells around the blister regenerated, and the adhesive fell off after a week. I bought six.

> *"I am not a smart man, particularly, but one day, at long last, I stumbled from the dark woods of my own, and my family's, and my country's past, holding in my hands these truths: that love grows from the rich loam of forgiveness; that mongrels make good dogs; that the evidence of God exists in the roundness of things. This much, at least, I've figured out. I know this much is true."*

– Wally Lamb, I Know This Much Is True

Day by day, I saw the same people. I met people from around Europe and a couple from New Zealand. None of them were Catholic; each was searching for something different—a couple from England and another from Austria, a French man and a German man, Frank.

Frank believed it was important not to wash his clothing, certainly not his socks. For him, bathing was optional; the less frequently, the more optimal.

He was mainly detached, hardly walked with anyone, and rarely spoke. He was also the most meditative.

People woke at different times, walked at different speeds, and, one by one, staggered into the next hostel. The six or seven of us planned for the next day, and each brought something different—pasta, bread, meat, and wine. Someone cooked, and we all ate and talked. We looked at the map to see where to meet the next day. One by one, we drifted off to sleep.

"With destruction comes renovation."

– Wally Lamb, I Know This Much Is True

Walking in October, the temperature was usually cold in the mornings and evenings. I layered on clothing, saw my breath as I started, and found a bar to sit in. I usually ordered coffee and toast. Orienting my mind was important, so I read and wrote. I revisited my guidebook.

Walking, I started shedding my outerwear as the sun rose. Half of the time, my muscles ached. I listened to Wally Lamb.

A week into my walk, I noticed changes. I was aware that my anxiety was lessening. I listened better to others. My mind was more intent. The food tasted better. My blisters hurt less. My dreams became more vivid. I wrote more and needed less.

Two weeks into my walk, I packed my boots and wore my sandals. I was eating less and eating better. I traded in old blisters for new ones. I felt lighter. My muscles were adapting, or I was adjusting to the pain.

At times, I felt alone, even sad. There was a part of my life that needed to change. I was stuck and needed to figure out why, what, or how. I was unsure of myself, not of the walk or the place or the people—just of the change that needed to happen, that was happening.

"What are our stories if not the mirrors we hold up to our fears?"

A few days before the end, as I approached Santiago, I finally broke. My body ached. My muscles screamed. New blisters bled. It was late morning. I sat on a bus bench, exhausted. My brain hurt. I cried.

A part of my life was leaving to make room for something new. The things I learned up to that part of my life would not help me in the next. Importance changed. Priorities shifted. Weight lifted. Decades later, I see this day as pivotal. I've had similar experiences, each a departure from the old to make way for the new. The transitions aren't fun, just necessary.

I finished my walk in Santiago, visited the cathedral, and received my certificate. I ate phenomenal food. I found a good hotel and took a long, hot shower. I slept in a real bed for days, it seemed.

I boarded my flight back home.

> "Epiphanies sometimes flash and flare for pilgrims, but there are also flickering moments of discovery on your journey, seen out of the corner of your eye."
>
> — Phil Cousineau. Art of Pilgrimage: The Seeker's Guide to Making Travel Sacred

The Camino did not end there.

While going through an experience like the Camino de Santiago, I understood others had not been. I was returning differently to the world I left, which remained the same. I was conscious for the first time that our return from travel has its impact and story.

Years later, while in Tibet, I saw a tour guide wearing a T-shirt with "pilgrim" written in Tibetan. Pilgrims who prayed and traveled, some from hundreds of miles away, came to Lhasa to pray. Traveling for an awakening is a real reason to go.

Occasionally, I meet people who want to walk the Camino de Santiago. I ask why and hear different answers. The answer is mostly an urge, something they do not know or fully understand. For some, it is because they are at the end of trying whatever they are doing.

> *"Your twin brother is, as you said, an abandoned house. If no one is home, then someone is missing. So, you grieve."*
>
> – Wally Lamb, I Know This Much Is True

The final outcome of my walk across Spain came from listening to Wally Lamb's book about his twin brother with schizophrenia. My own younger brother, a year and two weeks my junior, battles with schizophrenia. 'This Much I Know is True' stood as the solitary work I found that granted me an insightful comprehension of my brother's journey and the life he navigates.

I visit my brother when I can. I understand the concept of the abandoned house; at times, he is undoubtedly checked out. He has a great memory and still gets angry when wronged. He drinks a gallon or more of sweetened iced tea daily and smokes unfiltered cigarettes. He sits in a wheelchair after having spent most of his life walking six to eight hours per day, reading the bible out loud.

I hope this life is his pilgrimage.

TAKE AWAY: This was one of my top life experiences. In pain, I learned. The times my work was the most painful, I grew. No one taught me that. It was in relationship pain that I learned what was necessary. When we're stuck, it's the most challenging time to move. And, as the Chinese proverb says, "A journey of a thousand miles begins with a single step."

PART IV:
RETURNING

I'M A TRAVELING MAN. I'M A TRAVELING FOOL.

I'm a traveling man; I'm a traveling fool.

I make standby look fun and delays look cool.

I've been checked in, checked out, and crosschecked; bumped, booked, and over-booked.

Full-board or half-board. When I'm on board, I'm never bored.

Here I go. There I go. Catch me on the plane, and if I have an extra day or so, I'll probably take the train.

I've been over and out, out and about, in bed, well-fed, and back by popular demand.

I've been up and down, in and around, lost and found, grounded and stranded, embarked and barked at.

I still have places to go, bills to pay, letters to write, so I'm on my way.

I'm jet-lagged, jet-set, haven't met a jet I wouldn't like to board yet.

I'm always on board and always on time; if not in the lounge, you'll find me in line.

I take the long road home, the best way west and the least way east.

I've been here, I've been there,

I'm a pilgrim on the road to everywhere.

I'm a traveled man.

I traveled near and traveled far.

I packed light, slept tight, was out of mind and out of sight.

I certainly enjoyed the flight.

Good luck & good night!

DIVERSIONS

Lan Airlines, Santiago – Auckland

Most flights make it to where they're going the first time.

Flights occasionally divert or return to where they started because of bad weather, passenger issues, or aircraft problems. Cruise ships reposition because of storms. Trains are hard to turn around and have nearly zero chance of diverting. Planes just go somewhere else.

On a Valentine's Day trip to Paris, our plane diverted to Gander, Newfoundland, for a passenger who had a heart attack. I read that this is not uncommon, and Gander is the last airport from North America going toward Europe (and the first airport in North America from Europe). There was no gate, just stairs, so when the crew opened the airplane door, a blast of frigid air shot into the plane. An ambulance came to pick up the passenger, and after an hour, our plane took off again. In February, Paris is also cold, but I can't imagine Paris ever having an undesirable time to visit.

On another flight to Europe, I had a connection at JFK. The weather was terrible, and our plane diverted to Philadelphia. Our pilot was called "Captain Cowboy." His captain cap was a cowboy hat with a metal airline logo on the front. He was no doubt a classic of a foregone era. In a thick Texas drawl, he described flying through turbulence like "riding a bronco" and for us to "hang on" since he'd done both many times.

Nice. I missed my flight to Europe.

Other times, I landed in Austin instead of Dallas and Brisbane instead of Sydney. Each was due to the weather. Planes carry enough fuel to fly a few circles and then enough to go to another airport if planes are not landing at the original destination airport.

Another way to divert is after the pilot tries unsuccessfully to land the plane at the original airport and, as a result, must go somewhere else. The pilot might try to land once or twice. At Grand Cayman, the pilot attempted twice before diverting to Montego Bay, Jamaica. At Jacksonville and Orange County, other planes were on the runway, so the pilot flew past the airport and landed the second time.

Once our plane started to take off, we heard a loud pop from the middle engine, and the aircraft stopped. The pilot informed us that the engine "stalled," so after he restarted the engine, we took off like normal.

In New Orleans, we boarded the plane the evening before my birthday. The weather was hot and humid. We pulled from the gate, taxied to the runway, and stopped short. We waited and waited. The engines revved up, and we turned around. Due to weather problems at the other end, we returned to the gate, and the flight was canceled.

Waiting at the airport during flight delays is maddening. I am unaware of anyone who died waiting for their flight to leave, but I would not discount it either. So, during those times, I watch and wait. In New Orleans, I thought I would be sleeping in an airport seat on the just-mentioned flight since I was rebooked on a 7 a.m. flight. Not to be outdone, my colleague booked our hotel rooms. Most of the other passengers slept on the floor or in their seats.

Brake problems in Los Angeles and Orange County caused canceled flights. Thunderstorms in Denver and Miami, sick and disruptive passengers, and a sick pilot caused delays.

Once, we were well over the Pacific Ocean when a passenger took ill. The closest airport was three hours away, back where we started. Here is how that went:

Customs and Immigration, again.

Getting luggage, again.

Confusion.

Angry people.

An airport hotel.

Waiting 24 hours.

Returning to the airport.

Immigration.

Another plane.

Another crew.

Another day.

Unplanned landings, diversions, and turnarounds are metaphors for experiences we encounter. Each is unexpected. Our responses depend on how well we're trained and how well we're prepared, how we cope, how resilient we are, how we maneuver and manage, and how we respond or not.

The pilots in each scenario knew what to do and spent countless hours training, practicing, and preparing for these events.

And they performed flawlessly. We do, too, when we are trained, qualified, equipped, resilient, and responsive.

And sometimes, diversions are for the better.

As a student pilot, aeronautical concepts gelled in my mind in learning to fly. Traveling in three dimensions was like swimming; you go left or right and up and down. There is no actual roadway while flying, so constantly paying attention to direction (left, right, forward) and altitude (up and down) is super important. This was an entirely new venture, including getting the plane off the ground and the need to ultimately land safely, hopefully on a runway in one piece.

Words like thrust, drag, and lift took on new meanings. Speed made a plane go up and down, ultimately more than how fast the plane traveled. North, East, West, and South stayed the same, but directions became more technical. Like many GPS units, your car can point North or indicate the direction the road is going (up, down, left, or right). Both are right; they're just different.

So was the math around which runway to land on. I took my lessons at one of the busiest airports in the U.S. for student pilots. The airport where I learned to fly was the city my parents lived in when I was born, and it was founded by one of the most famous U.S. aviators after the Wright brothers, Glenn Curtiss.

The way planes land is straightforward. The airport tower controller assigns a runway where you land the plane depending on the wind direction. I was told to land on runway 27, heading West. I got the plane at the right altitude, pointed it toward the airport, and let the control tower know I was on my way.

A minute or two later, the tower controller asked me where I was. I told him. He acknowledged it. A few seconds later, I realized I was pointed at the wrong runway, not just a little. I was cutting across two other runways!

When I figured it out and asked to correct my mistake, the tower controller told me to land and meet with my instructor and the FAA. Ouch. Right airport. Wrong runway.

I thought of this years later when trying to "be" someone I was not or "do" something that didn't fit.

Right industry. Wrong persona.

Right trip. Wrong perspective.

Right destination. Wrong journey.

Right journey. Wrong destination.

Several thoughts come together...

(1) I relish the journey as much or more than the destination.

(2) I have been trained to envision an ideal life and mirror those who do what I imagine.

(3) I ask myself if I can make a living doing what I love.

(4) Would I still have a life?

I wanted to be Peter Greenberg even before I knew him.

Peter Greenberg is a television travel editor whom I first met at a travel conference for my company. My travel paled in comparison to Peter's. He lives in nice hotels. He travels for a living (11 million miles), gets paid well as far as I know, writes travel insider information, is known for what he does, and even has two or three (or more) suitcases in different parts of the world at the same time (he said it is better to send luggage via UPS or FedEx than check them under the plane). He taught us that many hotels allow frequent travelers to leave their clothes, clean them, and store them for the next time, although for me, it would seem strange to always wear the same clothes at the same destination for the same client. Same clothes or not, it sounds like the dream job to me.

I met Peter a year later at the same conference. While I would like to have a job like Peter Greenberg, I have also realized that my experience was different. I took a technology path, while Peter took a writing/journalism path. I'm sure Peter had other struggles proving his value to earn his position. He has paid the price and deserves what he does.

I see Peter from time to time at conferences. He loves what he does and makes a difference for people who want to minimize travel pain or anxiety. With Peter, I realized it's about paying the price.

Beijing – Lhasa on the train

> *"Travel is at its most rewarding when it ceases to be about your reaching a destination and becomes indistinguishable from living your life."*
>
> – Paul Theroux, Ghost Train to the Eastern Star, Ch 24

My two younger brothers and I are close in age and share most of what we grew up with. We shared schoolbooks, bicycles, toys, and a bedroom. At one time, our oldest brother and grandmother also shared our bedroom. Our beds became bunk beds. Our closet measured 4 feet by 4 feet, and nothing needed hanging. I can't think of anything we put in there.

Our white laminate dresser was communal. The dresser had to work for three or four kids. We had one drawer for long pants, one for short pants, one for T-shirts, two on the bottom for cold weather clothes, and the top left drawer kept our shared underwear and socks. For three boys, everything was communal - pants, t-shirts, socks, and underwear. Sometimes, I got tight underwear; other times, it was loose. It was the underwear lotto.

Decades later, I find myself on a two-day train trip from Beijing to Lhasa, Tibet, with my 20-something-year-old son, sharing a cabin with two bunk beds and two other people. There was room under the bottom bunk for storage, although not the sort of expanded suitcases most people bring. This is where the metal luggage sizers that no one uses at airports accurately describe the amount of space underneath the bottom bunk. We would have to store our stuff under the bunk or in a tiny compartment at the end of the top bunks over the hallway.

On this trip, what people couldn't cram into their cabin, they heaped at the end of the train car, near the bathrooms.

I met the writings of Paul Theroux while working for a train technology company. And, like many travelers, I gave train travel little thought. While speaking to an audience about taking the train from Los Angeles to Seattle and all the great features such as the coastline, the dining car, the bar car, the observation car, and my sleeper cabin, the response was something like, "Hey Jim, didn't they have flights?"

Theroux has written more than a dozen books on travel; the first is a classic, The Great Railway Bazaar, about his journey from London to Tokyo and his return by train, as much as he could. Within twenty pages, I felt I was on the train with him, hating every minute. Twenty pages later, I couldn't get off. Since then, I've consciously and deliberately taken the train or some other surface transportation wherever possible.

I thought, "I could be Paul Theroux."

And so, I found myself in the dining car traveling from Beijing to Lhasa, finishing Theroux's book on taking trains from Boston to Buenos Aires and then even further into Patagonia. Besides the first London to Tokyo trip, he did it a second time, took trains around China and Britain, traveled by boat around the Mediterranean and the South Pacific, and thumbed a ride from Cairo to Johannesburg when he couldn't take the train. I wondered why someone who seemed to hate train travel so much did it. But when I heard a recording of him speak, I learned to appreciate the man himself and that he wrote of the honest parts of travel and travel by train. Plus, he enjoys airplane travel the least.

Train travel is not always splendid. There are so many types of trains— commuter trains, private trains, long-distance trains, slow trains, fast trains, day trains, night trains, sleeper trains, new trains, and old trains. Trains around the world, Japan aside, are less on time, make more stops, have less air conditioning, have more breakdowns, and provide less personal space. Even in Japan, although they have 'pushers' who wear gloves to help the last few people board a crowded train, they do it with class.

New train stations are enclosed. They have more stores and better restaurants. Outside of these enclosed types of stations, train stations are open to the elements: rain, heat, snow, and ice. Some have stray dogs and people who live outdoors. Further from the larger stations, bathrooms are scarcer, are older, smell worse, and are cleaned less frequently. To cross over or under the tracks, train stations have a lot of stairs.

Back to our China trip, a hundred passengers in our car shared a Western toilet (the kind you sit on) and an Asian-style toilet (the kind you squat over) opening to the tracks below. No kidding. We also shared three sinks and a hot water spigot for making instant ramen or hot tea. We slept four in a cabin.

Six people were in a cabin in the next car, so one hundred and twenty people shared the two toilets and three sinks. The Western toilet water sloshed over the bowl rim when the train rocked back and forth, wetting the floor. At other times, the toilet stopped working, but people kept using it—a plus for the hole-in-the-floor toilet.

If the dining car was packed, we returned until there was an empty table. And if we missed the mealtime, we had to wait for the next mealtime. If we sat too long, the server kicked us out. One lady on our train waited nearly 24 hours before she got her mealtime right! But we shared what we had. The dining car, the attendants told us, was not a place to "hang out" if our cabin became claustrophobic. On most trains, experienced passengers bring food or use the onboard food preparation accommodation. We could smell it.

U.S. trains with smaller cabins have beds such that the passenger sleeps along the length of the car, while in other countries, the smaller cabins and beds sideways, across the rail car. The bottom bunks work as couches and cost more than the top bunks. Traveling to Lhasa, I lucked out by having a lower bunk that, when I sat down, allowed me to face forward.

The landscape was breathtaking. After leaving Beijing, the countryside appeared almost immediately. City after city, we made our way west to Tibet. After a day and a half, we crossed the Tanggula Pass—the world's highest rail track. Many long tunnels appeared to be broken rail sections on Google Maps.

Sitting on a stool in the hallway outside my cabin, watching the sunrise, I saw the yaks and the oxen feeding. Breath-smoke came from their nostrils in the cold mountain air. I shared the view with fellow travelers. People asked what I was reading, so I told them about Paul Theroux. I learned train travel is the most solo experience shared with other people, and we share what we have on the journey.

But I am not Paul Theroux. He is a fervent traveler and one of the most well-written authors.

I took a business path and fashioned myself after innovators and thought leaders. I tried being a better husband, a better father, a better colleague, a better friend, and a better traveler.

Through my travels, I've realized that I am not Peter Greenberg, Paul Theroux, Anthony Bourdain, or Pico Iyer. I didn't go through their lives nor have the same experiences. I read their books, listened to their speeches, and watched them on TV and YouTube, and I still learn from them.

Through each of them, I found a little more of myself.

I'm happy to be me, never traveling in a straight line.

TAKE AWAY: This is a long chapter, and I diverted even writing it. Life throws us diversions and transitions. Sometimes, we get stuck, or others around us get stuck. Much of my career was developing new products, services, and businesses. Generally, my work was disruptive to the staff. One of my favorite bosses helped me get through this, helped me get unstuck and back on track. She helped me see further than my challenge du jour. I learned to lend a hand to others who are at a barrier point.

GOING BACK

American Airlines, Nassau - Miami

The return home has its own set of unique emotions and experiences. With the serial traveler, home becomes a blur not just for the return but because each destination becomes common.

One Saturday, I was at Home Depot when I received a call that a good friend had passed away from a heart complication. I was stunned as this friend was not old and had received a favorable report after recent extensive testing. He was the CEO of a travel company, one of my clients. One of the board members called to ask if I was planning to attend the funeral and could attend a board meeting afterward. I agreed.

This would become a one-year commuting consulting role in the Bahamas. I lived near Los Angeles, and semi-weekly, I flew from the west coast of the U.S. to Miami, then on a connecting flight to Nassau. This friend ran a company with several lines of business, was a private pilot, and had his primary home on a different island. It was challenging.

As jobs and people go, he did a formidable job keeping it all together. Before his passing, I visited him two to three times a year for seven years. We discussed operating the company, managing the people, and adding new technologies. We met in other countries a few times to visit technology solutions companies. I knew his family and had dinner with them several times.

I always made my way back to the same airports in the same countries, and I felt more comfortable saying that the world was becoming my home. I was meeting the same people, going to the same restaurants, and taking the same flights.

Recently, I moved back to California after a seven-year absence. As I drove to the airport, I received a text message from one of the lounge staff who noticed my name on the flight. She asked me to stop by and say hello. It had been too long, it seemed, getting back.

My work had me to spend long periods working remotely, so I made sure never to travel in a straight line. To get to Miami, I flew via airports along the West Coast of the U.S.: San Diego, Los Angeles, San Francisco, and Seattle. Since these were overnight flights, longer flights meant more sleep and less groggy on arrival. I sat in my seat, usually in the exit row, took two PM pills, and fell asleep within twenty minutes.

It was great until one time when we got to the runway in Seattle and had to return to the terminal for a different aircraft. I drooled while half awake, waiting for the other aircraft to arrive. A better approach is to wait for the plane to take off. We arrived in Miami nearly six hours later. I ran to the lounge, took a quick shower, sprinted to the gate for Nassau like it was a shuttle, and arrived at work on time. I was back.

While working in the Bahamas, it became better as I got to know the people. I traveled around the islands and visited San Salvador, the island that was the first reported to be seen by Columbus. I met the staff on the different islands and ate lunch or dinner with many of them.

On my last trip to the Bahamas, I arrived in Nassau, aware that this would be my last trip working for this client. I paid attention to more details: the airport, the restaurants, the drive to and from the office, the staff, the office, and the homes. I thanked the staff at restaurants we visited differently. I saw the hotel room differently. As I was leaving, I wondered if I would return one day, what would be different, and what would be the same. Nassau felt like a second home.

The same happened during a commuting job in Brazil. I commuted to São Paulo and Porto Alegre in the south. Since most flights to Brazil are overnight, I took the day flight to Miami. Different staff, different routines, and different times. Same planes, same wait, same airports, and same sleep pattern.

What's it like to feel you won't go back somewhere? How about London, Paris, or New York? Or home?

I have a habit of counting steps. From the jet bridge door to the airplane door at DFW Terminal A, gate 30, it is 42 steps; from the airplane (LAX BA flight) to customs is 625; from room 334 to the lobby door at the Omni Boston is 85 steps down the street. Over and over, I count. It may be because I want to know how many steps it would take if I could not see because of a fire or other reason.

I've gone to the same places over and over. Nassau, Paris, London, Boston, Los Angeles, Dallas-Fort Worth, Chicago, Laguardia, Miami, John Wayne - Santa Ana - Orange County (all the same airport).

After traveling to the same destination several times, I felt like I belonged to each place. I check out of a hotel and know someone else will likely stay in the same room that night. I get off a plane and know someone else will sit in my seat in an hour. Someone else will take my spot at a restaurant with the same server, holding the same menu.

When I visit a place, I wonder when I will return. I appreciate the sights, the food, the language, the smells, the customs, and the people.

I want to remember a place when I look at a boarding pass.

The cycle of comings and goings never seems to end.

And that's the way life seems.

TAKE AWAY: Often, we see the end of a project, place, or relationship up ahead. Toward this end, our vigor and interest may wane. We may be coming from a place of pain, tiredness, or exhaustion. This is a great time to consider what you want to remember.

CREATING YOUR EPIPHANIES

Southwest Airlines, Dallas–Santa Ana

> *"The adventure that you're ready for is the one that you're living."*
>
> – Joseph Campbell

Sitting at the harbor in Dana Point, California, I have a dozen thoughts on beginning and writing this chapter. As a professional strategist, there is more than one answer to most questions and more than one way to get there.

The short answer, "Jim, do you believe we can create an epiphany?" is yes. It is less about creating than about paying attention.

In the book Life is in the Transitions, Bruce Fiedler writes, *"The world no longer adheres to predictable, linear mandates. Instead, life is filled with chaos and complexity, periods of order and disorder, linearity and non-linearity. In place of steady lines, observers now see loops, spirals, wobbles, fractals, twists, tangles, and turnabouts."* This is also a picture of travel. In the transitionary periods, the goal is to become more aware of and learn from life's happenings.

In my work understanding ultra-luxury and well-traveled travelers, the multiple "trip of a lifetime" concept was at the forefront. It was not just about paying attention to the traveler but knowing what was beyond their imagination. I call this the Aspirational Horizon, which applies in or out of travel.

The Aspirational Horizon has a view as far as the individual can 'see.' Imagine the horizon wherever you are, as far as you can see. Now, conceptualize that as an event or experience—maybe a promotion, a local trip, or a project completion. As much as the individual can grasp, whatever is sought after is their horizon.

As they reach the horizon, the concept is that the person will climb higher and see further, travel further, climb, and complete more. At a membership company I worked at, many members could not afford to travel, so when they found something for under $100, they bought it. This was their Aspirational Horizon. A $100 trip was as far as they could imagine with their means or time. My work was to get them to take a trip, and the next time, they would go further, upgrade perhaps, bring a friend, and spend more.

Is it possible to create an epiphany, find some understanding, fulfillment, or answer, and for travel to be the conduit? I believe so. As I wrote at the beginning of this book, epiphanies happen when we least expect them and need them the most. Sometimes, they appear out of pain, boredom, conflict, strain, and indecision.

Incidentally, each of these happens during travel. When I walked across Spain, my emotions heightened daily. After a week or ten days, my awareness became clearer. Dreams became more lucid. Conversations deepened. People became more meaningful. Important life decisions revealed themselves.

Is it possible to plan a journey knowing something unusual will happen before, during, or after you return? I believe so. The unfamiliarity of travel, even routine, creates scenarios for the unforeseen. Weather, mechanical issues, baggage, other passengers, lines, and meetings are each opportunity.

Is it possible to yearn for something so much that the yearning becomes the journey? I believe so. In her profoundly soulful book, The Holy Longing, Connie Zweig describes a longing as something possibly never attained.

Is it possible to create an epiphany?

Even as we plan our journey, the mysterious happens, and we find that our purpose or need is being fulfilled. I remember a story about someone who had a desperate need. They wrote and rewrote their prayer with increased meaning. With pain, they rehearsed their prayer, imagining a favorable result. Days passed, but before they prayed the words, their prayer came to be. They felt cheated.

Can we pre-create such an event? I believe so. And then, we can enjoy our trip more.

TAKE AWAY: I've often seen people quit just before the breakthrough. I know I have as well. When is the right time to walk away, and when is the right time to push forward? What are the considerations for each? Think about your own challenges - either way, there is a breakthrough.

TRAVEL EPIPHANIES

When we're ready but possibly least expect it, we glimpse something new that grabs our attention. A glimmer. An idea. A challenge. A struggle. An awareness. A twist. A smile. A pain. Someone else's pain.

Pay attention.

What is the experience saying to you?

TAKE AWAY: Small experiences add up. What you need right now may be reflecting a path forward. And, at times, these small experiences grow until there is no other option.

HOW WILL WE REMEMBER?

Cathay Pacific Airlines, Hong Kong–Tokyo

> *"How will you remember to remember when you return home?"*
>
> – Phil Cousineau, The Art of Pilgrimage: A Seekers Guide to Making Travel Sacred

What's a boarding pass?

A last name.

A first name.

A getting-on point.

A getting-off point.

A date.

A reservation number.

A loyalty identifier.

But really, what else is a boarding pass?

A record of passage from one place to another?

The representation of a contract to board the plane, ship, or bus?

A rite of passage?

Before a boarding pass became a digital artifact on our phones, a boarding pass was a piece of paper. Before that, a gate agent wrote the seat number on the ticket jacket with a felt-tip marker (watch the movie Airport to get an idea). Later, they graduated to seat stickers.

I have a few ticket jackets with a seat number written on them.

As I write this, the boarding pass is quickly becoming my face in a camera at the airline check-in, airport security line, boarding gate, and Immigration and Customs, a relic of a soon-bygone era.

I've saved many of my paper boarding passes and still keep the ones on my phone. I know others who hold onto their boarding passes. My son saves boarding passes. Friends long gone kept boarding passes—their children call to ask if I want them.

Why did they save their boarding passes?

"Hi, Jim. My father died. I know you two were close. He has a box of travel stuff and a boarding pass from a flight on Concorde. Would you like it?"

I love boarding passes. I've used boarding passes as bookmarks. I find them in books read long ago, a reminder of when I read them. I've used boarding passes as playing cards, as dominos, or to tell stories to young people who have never seen them.

What memories do boarding passes hold?

A special trip?

A visit to a friend?

An airline long gone?

To a place long ago forgotten?

Next to a seatmate who bared their soul, or to whom we bared our soul?

It could be a harrowing experience we lived through.

To some, boarding passes are sacred, and the memories have become more valuable than the cost of the trip itself.

It feels like I've traveled more than I've been home. When my son was growing up, his favorite present when I returned from a trip was a boarding pass. Not candy. No pictures. It wasn't a toy. It was a boarding pass.

A first-class boarding pass was worth more than a coach boarding pass. A foreign boarding pass was worth more than a U.S. one. An unfamiliar city was gold. He lined up chairs and put boarding passes on each seat to create his own experience for whatever he imagined the journey was.

"What did the airport look like?"

"Where did you get your boarding pass?"

"What was the boarding process like?"

"How clean was the plane?"

"How new was the seat?"

"How small (or big) was the lavatory?"

"Did they serve a drink and food?"

"How attentive were the flight attendants?"

For my son, the trip mattered most. Whether I flew to Little Rock or London— the questions were the same. A boarding pass was the evidence.

What is the experience we have when we travel? Some people suffer "the journey" to their destination, while others could not care less where they're going—they're just happy to be going. Seemingly, people's views of travel are often their views of life… journey or destination.

People travel for all kinds of reasons—for business, vacation, funerals, to fight a foreign war, to visit families, to find a lost love, to get away from their kids, to get away from their parents, to get away from their self, or to find their self. Possibly, as Carl Jung put it, "We leave to come back."

Watching people travel and being around travelers so frequently, I see and experience many emotions: happy, sad, lonely, contemplative, melancholy, desperate, angry, afraid, excited, patient, and impatient. Recently, I saw a herd of business travelers rushing to the gate, driven to get aboard, get their luggage stowed, and ensure they had seat space. I saw myself in them.

Experience and what others experience while traveling are intriguing to me. Those experiences, whatever they are, can be rich and deep with meaning— even a simple business trip if we pay attention to our thoughts and feelings.

Boarding passes tell us about a journey, the memories, and maybe the accompanying experiences. The first time to a new city or country. A trip to meet a future spouse or significant other. The first glimpse of a monument, a building, a mountain, the beach, and the ocean.

Equally, a boarding pass is a reminder of not being somewhere that mattered. A boarding pass to Nairobi reminds me of missing my daughter's high school graduation. A friend reminded me of missing her mother's last breath but keeps the boarding pass in her wallet. Our boarding pass is the evidence we traveled and our experience - with the ticket counter agent, the security guard, the gate agent, the seatmate, the weather, or a cab driver. All we have left is paper or a QR code on our phone.

I have four expired passports, including one from the Camino de Santiago.

And I have boxes of boarding passes.

> *"You knew these things about people and places before you left home, but you had forgotten them. This journey reminded you of the sacred rhythms. How will you remember to remember when you return home?"*

> — Phil Cousineau, The Art of Pilgrimage: A Seekers Guide to Making Travel Sacred

TAKE AWAY: Over the years, I've accumulated artifacts of my journey (singular) and journeys (plural) - work, personal, and travel. One of my favorite travelers is Abraham, from the Middle East. As a wanderer in the desert, he had many profound walking experiences, even epiphanies. He took what was around, generally rocks, and built places of remembrance to remember what happened when he passed by at some future point, or others could recall when they passed by. Remember what is important to you. Create something to remember them with. These are what you will return to one day.

GULLIBLE'S TRAVELS BY FRED W. MENGE

TV programs are appealing
I don't like to hurt their feelings
Makes me feel that I'm square dealing
When I buy what they are wheeling
If I don't, I feel I'm stealing
so I must buy, though I'm reeling
as I've many cures for healing
stacked up high from floor to ceiling.

I have drops for runny nose,
pads galore for calloused toes,
scads of pills when tension shows,
also those when stomach goes.
Several if I fail to doze,
aids for constipation woes,
others when a headache grows
and many more for ulcer's foes.

Hair oils should I chase a dame,
Pep-ups when my hair is lame,
others if I'm really game,
and one makes rivals hide in shame.
Another has a sexy name
and one that gives me grayless fame

there's one that boasts the greatest claim
it even makes a tiger tame.

As sporting programs I love dear,
Naturally, I'm stocked with beer,
so many brands from far and near
that I can't see those in the rear.
Too many now I have a fear,
that should the agents care to peer
down in my cellar, I would hear
the judge say, "Buddy, take a year."

My garage stores pet food now
more different brands than laws allow
enough to make me wipe my brow,
I must get rid of them somehow.
Since cases broke and scattered chow
my neighbors are all in a row;
all day long, the dogs Bow Wow
and every night, the cats meow.

I've soaps of all kinds by the score
piled up back of every door.
There's some for dishes that you pour,
and some for doing laundry chores.
There's those enjoyed in shower's roar
and one that was a dove before,
but I don't need those for the floor
'Cause I can't find it anymore.

I've beauty aids for lady fair
stacked up nearly everywhere.
Cigarettes in cartons share
with cereals, the cellar stair.
I've shirts and clothes of wash and wear
and toothpaste that give teeth a glare.

I've many brands of coffee rare,
there's not a piece of floor that's bare.

Now no more space, how I regret,
I wonder why, how did I let
those T.V. ad men make me get
so many things, so deep in debt.
But worst of all, what makes me sweat,
no more can I watch Dave and Chet
as back of all this stuff is yet
hidden now, my T.V. set.